GARDENING
PROJECTS FOR KIDS

GARDENING
PROJECTS FOR KIDS

Fantastic ideas for making things, growing plants and flowers, and attracting wildlife, with 60 practical projects and 500 photographs

Jenny Hendy

southwater

This edition is published by Southwater,
an imprint of Anness Publishing Ltd,
Blaby Road, Wigston, Leicestershire LE18 4SE
email: info@anness.com

www.southwater.com; www.annesspublishing.com

If you like the images in this book and would like to investigate using them for publishing, promotions or advertising, please visit our website www.practicalpictures.com for more information.

Publisher: Joanna Lorenz
Senior Editors: Lucy Doncaster and Emma Clegg
Designer: Lisa Tai
Photographer: Howard Rice
Models: Aidan, Alyson, Anna, Ashley, Christian, Eleanor, Grace, Holly, Imogen, Jenny, Jessica, Juliet, Kirsty, Lorna, Lucy D., Lucy I., Lucy P., Matthew R., Matthew T., Michael, Rhys, Siani and Viv
Production Controller: Bessie Bai

Ethical trading policy

At Anness Publishing we believe that business should be conducted in an ethical and ecologically sustainable way, with respect for the environment and a proper regard to the replacement of the natural resources we employ.

As a publisher, we use a lot of wood pulp in high-quality paper for printing, and that wood commonly comes from spruce trees. We are therefore currently growing more than 750,000 trees in three Scottish forest plantations: Berrymoss (130 hectares/ 320 acres), West Touxhill (125 hectares/305 acres) and Deveron Forest (75 hectares/185 acres). The forests we manage contain more than 3.5 times the number of trees employed each year in making paper for the books we manufacture.

Because of this ongoing ecological investment programme, you, as our customer, can have the pleasure and reassurance of knowing that a tree is being cultivated on your behalf to naturally replace the materials used to make the book you are holding.

Our forestry programme is run in accordance with the UK Woodland Assurance Scheme (UKWAS) and will be certified by the internationally recognized Forest Stewardship Council (FSC). The FSC is a non-government organization dedicated to promoting responsible management of the world's forests. Certification ensures forests are managed in an environmentally sustainable and socially responsible way. For further information about this scheme, go to www.annesspublishing.com/trees

Previously published as part of a larger volume, *The Ultimate Step-by-Step Kid's First Gardening Book*

Publisher's note

Although the advice and information in this book are believed to be accurate and true at the time of going to press, neither the authors nor the publisher can accept any legal responsibility or liability for any errors or omissions that may have been made nor for any inaccuracies nor for any loss, harm or injury that comes about from following instructions or advice in this book. All children need to work with adult guidance and supervision and it is the parent's or carer's responsibility to ensure the child is working safely.

Contents

Having fun in the garden

For active kids gardens provide endless adventure. With a little guidance, some basic equipment and a few plants, kids can also have fun growing things in the garden, transforming even the smallest outdoor space into a blooming oasis they can be proud of.

▶ *It's really satisfying picking bright flowers that you have grown in the garden.*

The great outdoors

Green spaces give kids the chance to let off steam, to play physical, outdoor games and to be carefree. Games created in the open air are often different to those played indoors, because the fluctuating environment stimulates young imaginations. What is more, the seasons, weather and daily pattern of light and dark affect plants and creatures in many tangible ways. This changing landscape is fascinating for kids, and a valuable learning experience.

Why should kids garden?

Before the massive growth of urban areas and automated transport, children would have been more attuned to the natural world around them. Sadly, today, it is easy for children to become cut off from nature. Modern living keeps us all indoors for longer than is healthy in terms of body, mind and spirit. Advances in technology have done nothing to help foster a connection with nature and many children are reluctant to break away from their favourite TV programme or computer game to venture outdoors, especially in cold or damp weather.

▲ *Gardening jobs can be fun and learning about plants can be interesting – maybe you can have a pot of your own to tend.*

▲ *Enjoy eating homegrown fruits such as blackberries.*

▲ *Attract birds by giving them regular supplies of food.*

Being able to see the sky and experience daylight directly, to breathe in fresh air and to smell flower perfumes or the damp earth after rain, and to become aware of the natural world, all help us to reconnect with nature on a primal level. Research has shown that children who are able to play in and explore gardens and green spaces in an unstructured way are better able to remain grounded and in tune with nature as adults. Not surprisingly, this ability helps us to cope better with stress. And children who have positive experiences of gardening and outdoor play and who are encouraged to observe nature often return to these pastimes as adults even after a break of several years.

So it falls to parents to stimulate their kids by getting them out in the fresh air and showing them how to discover the interesting things around them, in the garden and beyond. So entice them out with one of the projects in this book and be prepared to join in and offer plenty of help and encouragement!

Designing a children's garden

There are many kinds of garden, large and small, wild or manicured, and some are better suited to the needs of children. Whatever kind of garden you have, don't worry, because any open space where plants are grown can encourage an interest in gardening. This could be a tiny flower- or vegetable-filled balcony or a small bed or collection of pots in a courtyard. If you give children their own plot or pots it will feel like a special treat, and helps to teach responsibility. With very young ones, you'll need to act as backup, doing extra watering and pest control so that the results of their efforts don't disappoint.

◀ It's fun to try rooting all kinds of cuttings in water, including houseplants, patio plants, herbs and shrubs. Some, such as African violets, will root from a single leaf! The one shown here is mint.

▼ There's a whole other world to discover outdoors in your garden and further afield. Why not keep a record of the plants, insects and animals you find so you can see how the seasons affect them.

ADAPTING A GARDEN FOR CHILDREN

There are plenty of steps you can take to make a garden more child-friendly and stimulating. Try the following where space allows:

✔ Create lots of hidden or secret corners using evergreen shrubs, rigid screens or brushwood or bamboo roll attached to posts or canes (stakes).

✔ Consider making a raised platform or build a boardwalk or walkway to wind through plantings.

✔ Introduce a see-through division using trellis or robust plants, such as bamboo, to protect delicate plantings from an area used for ball games.

✔ Have as large a lawn or open grassy area as you can manage. Sow or turf with a hard-wearing grass or grass/clover mix. Any lawn areas, but especially weedy ones, are good for wildlife too!

✔ If you have room, plant a mini woodland or copse. Set the saplings relatively close together for more instant results and greater potential for play. Silver birch (*Betula pendula*) is ideal.

✔ Leave wild margins or relatively uncultivated areas with long grass, weeds and wild flowers to encourage insects, butterflies and birds.

✔ Grow fruit and vegetables – you don't need a vegetable plot as such, just a few tubs on the patio will suffice. Include fruits that can be picked and eaten straight from the plant, such as tomatoes, raspberries and strawberries.

✔ Grow big, bright colourful blooms – don't worry about colour schemes, especially when the kids are little – as well as larger-than-life foliage plants to tower over children.

✔ Buy a few child-size tools and a small wheelbarrow so that young children can garden alongside you and help move around plants, pots, material for the compost heap etc.

▲ Use an eye glass to see what's happening close up.

▲ Help with all kinds of gardening jobs.

having fun in the garden

How to use this book

This book is intended to be used as an inspirational sourcebook by parents and children. It is hoped that the projects here will promote further adventures in gardening and wildlife spotting as kids grow in confidence with their new-found knowledge.

▶ *You will get a kick out of raising plants from seed.*

How to garden

The first parts of this book look at how to approach growing things in the garden, explains some of the common gardening terms and jargon, and how to stay safe when working with plants, as well as the essential tools and equipment you will need. This is followed by some colourful and fascinating facts about plants and soil that are presented in a way that is really easy to understand. We look at how plants grow and what they need to thrive, as well as the seasonal variations in a garden and its regular growth patterns, including features showing the lifecycle of a flower and a leaf. Gardening is undoubtedly one of the very best ways for children to learn about the cycle of life, to discover where food comes from and to become aware of the wonders of the natural world around them.

A wealth of ideas

There then follow five practical, hands-on chapters including Flower Power, which is about how to grow beautiful blooms; Fork to Fork, an introduction to cultivating fruits, vegetables and herbs; and Garden

▲ *Gardening and exploring alongside an adult is the best way to teach children safety in the garden and further afield.*

Gardening safely

Children develop at different rates and only parents or guardians will know when their kids are ready to be introduced to using specific tools or are able to help with certain jobs. Working alongside a grown-up and having a go at something (under close supervision at first) is a great way for children to learn safe practices and to gain the skills needed for greater independence, although continuing adult guidance will be required.

Some of the projects in this book use knives, scissors or garden cutting tools, such as secateurs and pruners, or a saw, hammer and nails. Adult supervision is always required when using these, no matter how old or experienced the child, and more help will be required for younger children. Pictures showing how to do something dangerous, which will require adult help or supervision, have been highlighted with icons, shown below:

 the task being shown uses sharp or dangerous implements, such as secateurs, scissors, hammers or spades. Adult help may be required to do the step or, at the very least, supervise children very carefully.

the task being shown involves moving or lifting something heavy, using heat or a dangerous substance, or doing something difficult. Adult help may be required to do the step or, at the very least, supervise children very carefully.

Safari, which examines many interesting ways to encourage and observe all kinds of exciting creatures. Many of the Crafty Ideas offer handmade projects for the garden that can also be done indoors if it's cold outside, and there is a whole chapter of Rainy Day Gardening projects, ranging from making miniature gardens to growing funky houseplants.

Choosing a project

When selecting a project, first check the coloured strip across the top of the page to see if it's the right time of year to start the project and how long it might take to make or grow. In order to help you see how easy or difficult a project is, we've also added a star rating system, which works as follows:

★ = the project is 'easy as ABC'. All children from 5 to 12 should be able to tackle these, and there isn't any cutting or specialist tool use involved so it's nice and safe for younger kids. Adult supervision may still be required.

★★ = you should 'give it a try'! There might be some cutting or more manual dexterity involved and children might have to keep tending to the project over a longer period of time. With parental supervision and occasional help, most children will be able to enjoy them.

★★★ = the project is 'nice and challenging'. These are designed for older children and perhaps kids who already have some gardening experience and are ready to try some more advanced techniques. Adult supervision will still always be required for any steps involving dangerous implements.

▲ *You can grow your own vegetables in patio pots, like these radicchio plants – but you'll need to keep them well watered!*

Getting organized

It's worth reading the brief introduction to the projects, which shows you what you can achieve. So that you know you have everything to hand, use the 'you will need' list to draw all the materials together. There is also a separate 'plant list' with common and Latin names, making it easier to shop for plants or seeds.

▲ *Wearing gloves, hand-pick and relocate caterpillars.*

▲ *Get your hands dirty harvesting the potato crop.*

You may already have most things needed for the projects and, if not, the materials specified are often inexpensive and easy to obtain. Many can be sourced from recycled items. You might also consider substituting bits and pieces of equipment with similar elements already in your supplies. And, rather than buying all the plants for a scheme, why not work with the children to see what seedlings, cuttings and divisions might be grown to prepare for planting later in the season or next year? It is both fun and economical.

Preparing to garden!

After ensuring that the garden is as risk-free as it can reasonably be, children should have as much freedom within its boundaries as possible. Dig out plenty of old clothes so that they can run around and get as mucky as they like. The following pages cover the essentials of preparing your young gardeners or wildlife explorers for outdoor fun and helping them stay safe and secure.

Playing safe

Compared to the great outdoors, gardens represent a relatively safe haven for children. There are a few things that you can do to lessen the risk of accidents. Make preparing to garden or play outdoors a simple routine with easy-to-follow rules and boundaries.

▶ *It is important to wear sensible clothes when you are gardening.*

Safety first
reducing risk in the garden

Before you allow children to roam free in a garden, you need to carry out a basic risk assessment, especially when moving to a new house:

- ✘ Never leave young children unattended in the garden.
- ✔ Look for open or poorly secured manhole or cellar covers (or crawl-space entries) and make sure they are secure before letting children out.
- ✔ Check that all boundaries are impenetrable and gates are locked.
- ✔ Where young children, including friends of your own kids, are likely to use the garden, securely fence off or drain ponds.
- ✔ Look out for sharp objects, including barbed wire, around the garden boundary and consider removing or relocating plants with sword-like leaves (e.g. yucca, agave) as well as prickly or thorny plants, such as roses and barberry (*Berberis* spp.).
- ✔ Make sure your family is up to date with their tetanus immunizations because even a small cut or thorn prick can introduce the disease.
- ✔ Put tops on canes (stakes) to protect eyes.
- ✔ Children love to climb so secure steep drops, such as those next to decks, retaining walls and steps, with guardrails.
- ✔ Lock away tools as well as chemicals, including outdoor paints and preservatives, lawnmower fuel, oils, lubricants and fertilizers.
- ✔ If there are pets around, check the garden for any faeces and pick it up and dispose of it on a regular basis. Stress to children that they must not touch it, and always ensure they wash their hands as soon as they come in.

Local knowledge
Talk to your children about any specific local hazards that may come into the garden from the outside. These might include aggressive ant species, wasp or hornet nests, snakes and other poisonous or biting creatures as well as wild and cultivated plants that can sting or potentially cause allergic reactions. If these could be a problem, adults should be extra vigilant with their supervision.

Summer sun
Children are particularly vulnerable to damage from the sun, especially those with fair or freckly skin, or with blonde or red hair. The results of sunburn are not only painful but can also potentially store up health problems for later life.

1 Apply specially formulated children's sunscreens with a high UVA and UVB protection. Reapply often and limit the amount of time spent in midday sun.
2 Provide shaded rest areas under trees, in tents or under temporary canopies. Offer drinks to keep kids hydrated.
3 Put on a brimmed hat. Boys will often be reluctant but could be persuaded with a cowboy stetson, Indiana Jones-style explorer's hat or pirate's tricorn.
4 Cover up with a T-shirt or long-sleeved shirt.

▲ *Long-sleeved T-shirts help protect skin from the sun.*

▲ *Make sure you apply high factor sun cream frequently.*

Safety first
poisonous and irritant plants

Most plants used in this book are safe to handle, unless consumed. If you suspect your child has eaten something poisonous, take them straight to the hospital emergency department with a sample of the plant. Don't try to make them vomit. Never grow *Ricinus communis* (castor oil plant) in a garden used by children as it is highly toxic. Some plants have potentially irritant hairs, or sap that may react with sunlight, and may irritate skin. *Ruta graveolens* (rue) is one of the worst examples of the latter type and contact can require emergency medical treatment.

The list below doesn't include wild plants or mushrooms/toadstools, whose dangers children should also be made aware of. Neither is it comprehensive, so if you are unsure, check first.

* **Angel's trumpets**
  Brugmansia spp. and cvs.
* **Castor oil plant**
  Ricinus communis
* **Cherry laurel**
  Prunus laurocerasus
* **Daffodil** (may irritate skin)
  Narcissus
* **Delphinium**
* **Foxglove**
  Digitalis
* **Ivy**
  Hedera spp.
* **Laburnum**
  Laburnum anagyroides
* **Lily of the valley**
  Convallaria majalis
* **Mezereon**
  Daphne mezereum
* **Monkshood**
  Aconitum
* **Portugal laurel**
  Prunus lusitanica
* **Rhubarb**
  (toxic leaves)
  Rheum raponticum
* **Rue** (may irritate skin)
  Ruta graveolens
* **Spurge** (may irritate skin)
  Euphorbia
* **Tobacco plant**
  Nicotiana
* **Yew**
  Taxus baccata

▲ *Rue can irritate skin.*

▲ *Castor oil plant is toxic.*

Hands and feet

Where possible children should be encouraged to garden without gloves as this increases their sensory experience. However, when using digging or cutting tools or handling prickly or irritant plants, they should put on a pair of children's gardening gloves. Ask your children to wash their hands when they come in from the garden, especially before eating, and discourage nail biting or finger licking when outdoors.

Wellington (rubber) boots or stout shoes protect toes from accidents with tools or sharp objects in the soil, so should always be worn when gardening.

Safety first
using tools and equipment

Showing children how to use tools properly helps prevent accidents and makes gardening more rewarding. Encourage them to clean, tidy away or hang up their garden tools and equipment after use, so they are out of the way and will last longer.

- ✔ Wear thick gardening gloves when using digging or cutting tools. Adult supervision is always required when using these tools.
- ✔ Distribute the load in a wheelbarrow evenly.
- ✘ Don't overload wheelbarrows or garden trolleys, and use one that is a suitable size.
- ✘ Don't try to lift too much soil on a fork or spade when digging. Adult supervision is required, and help should be given.
- ✘ Don't use secateurs or pruners unsupervised and always leave them closed with the safety catch on. Younger children should not use them.
- ✘ Never leave rakes, hoes or other long-handled tools lying on the ground.

▲ *Put away tools.*

▲ *Take care when digging.*

Useful gardening terms

When you first start gardening some of the words and phrases you'll hear may sound rather confusing. Don't be put off though. We've explained some of the more commonly used terms for you here, and any that aren't listed will be in the dictionary or on the internet.

▶ *You will already know some gardening terms, but perhaps not others.*

Annual This is a plant that grows from seed, flowers, makes more seed and then dies, all in one year. 'Hardy annuals' are easy to grow from seed sown straight in the ground and 'half-hardy' annuals, which need extra warmth to germinate and grow in spring, can't be planted outdoors until the risk of frosty weather has passed. Usually this is early summer.

Bulb This is an underground swelling at the base of a plant's stem that stores food as well as a tiny flowering plant, ready to bloom in the following year.

Chitting In this method for encouraging seed potatoes to start growing, you place them in a light place with their 'eyes' or buds uppermost and allow them to sprout. This is called chitting.

Compost Used frequently in the garden, compost is the dark brown, crumbly rotted-down remains of plant material that is worked into the ground to improve the soil and help grow bigger, better flowers, fruits and vegetables. Compost also describes the bags of potting soil (soil mix) bought to fill pots and baskets.

Crock This is a piece of broken clay pot or tile put into the bottom of a planting container to cover the drainage hole(s) so that soil doesn't block them. You can also use stones or broken-up Styrofoam plant trays.

Cutting A shoot tip, piece of stem or sometimes the root of a plant, cuttings are put into pots or trays of compost (soil mix), or, for easy plants, jars of water. With luck, these pieces make new roots and eventually a whole new plant develops.

Deadheading This is the action of removing old or fading flowers by cutting or pinching them off with thumb and index finger, to prevent the plant from making seeds. Annual plants may stop flowering altogether if allowed to form seed-heads and most plants look better with old flowers removed.

Deciduous This term describes shrubs, trees and climbers that lose their leaves in autumn and grow fresh leaves in spring.

Evergreen Trees, shrubs, climbers and perennial plants that keep their leaves even through the colder winter months are called evergreens.

Fertilizer Another word for plant food, fertilizer comes in different forms, ranging from well-rotted manure to granular or liquid feeds.

Germination When a seed swells with water and starts to grow into a baby plant, unfolding its seed leaves and pushing out its root, this is called

▲ *Borage is an annual plant loved by bees.*

▲ *Bulbs are little time capsules containing sleeping plants.*

▲ *Compost is made from rotted-down plant waste.*

▲ *Add granular fertilizer straight to the soil.*

▲ Staking a young tree will support it until it gets stronger.

▲ When a shoot appears, your seed has germinated.

▲ Lemon verbena is a deciduous shrub.

▲ Pollination is carried out by insects, such as bumble-bees.

germination. You can see germination in action when you put bean seeds or sprinklings of cress seed on damp blotting paper (*see page 28*).

Hardening off The shoots or leaves of young plants grown from seeds or cuttings indoors or in the greenhouse are too soft at first to be planted straight out in the garden. They must be gradually introduced to cooler outdoor temperatures, stronger light levels and breezier conditions in order to toughen them up. This process is called hardening off and takes two to three weeks. A glass or plastic **cold frame** is often used as a halfway house. Lightly shaded at first, the lid or vents are raised by increasing amounts in the day but are closed at night.

Manure Usually cow or horse dung mixed with straw bedding, this is left to rot down to make garden fertilizer. It's also a great soil improver and mulch. The heap takes about three to four years to break down.

Mulch A thick layer of material, such as chipped tree bark, put on to the soil around plants to help smother weeds. Mulches, such as well-rotted manure or garden compost, also help to keep soils, such as sandy loams, from drying out in summer and these types also provide plant fertilizers.

Naturalize Particularly important for the wild garden look, naturalizing is where certain bulbs or perennials that spread and multiply easily are planted to form large, natural-looking patches in lawns, long grass or the ground under trees.

Perennial This term describes non-woody flowering or foliage plants that are evergreen or more usually **herbaceous**, i.e. they die down in winter and regrow from ground level in spring. The hardy herbaceous perennials as a group contain most of the common border flowers.

Pinching out Carefully nipping off the shoot tip or growing point of a plant, often a seedling or young plant, is called pinching out. It encourages the plant to produce side shoots and become more bushy.

Plunging This is an easy way of thoroughly wetting the roots of a potted specimen before planting. Fill a bucket of water and hold the plant pot under the water surface until the air bubbles stop.

Pollination Bees and other insects transfer male pollen to the female part of the flower – a process called pollination. This allows seed to be produced and fruits to ripen.

Pricking out (Potting on) When a tray of seedlings starts to grow their first set of true leaves and are large enough to handle, each baby plant is moved to another container to give them more room to grow. This is called pricking out. The seedlings are delicate and the tiny roots should be lifted out of the compost (soil mix) or cuttings (seed-starting) mix with the end of a pencil or stick while holding a leaf for support.

Propagation This technique makes more plants and includes several methods, such as sowing seed, taking cuttings, divisions or rooting offshoots or runners. Seeds and cuttings may be put in a **propagator**, which keeps the compost (soil mix) or cuttings (seed-starting) mix warm and moist to encourage germination or rooting.

Pruning Cutting off parts of a woody plant, such as a shrub or climber, to improve its shape, get rid of diseased or damaged stems and branches, or to encourage flowering and fruiting, is called pruning.

Staking This involves using a stick or bamboo cane to prop up a plant and prevent it being damaged by wind or rain or falling over because it is top-heavy.

Tools and equipment

You can now find quite a wide range of gardening tools especially designed to suit the height and body size of younger gardeners. They aren't as heavy as tools for grown-ups and some have adjustable handles so that you can keep using them as you grow.

▶ *Pick tools that are just the right size for you to use.*

Trowel

One of the most important tools in any garden, a trowel is a mini hand-held spade that is used for making small holes and digging up weeds. They come in various sizes, so make sure you choose one that fits comfortably in your hand and is not too heavy for you to use. They need to be sturdy enough to handle a bit of digging. Take care when using.

▲ *Trowel*

Hand fork

There are two main types of hand fork: angled ones and flat ones. The angled type is best for loosening the soil between plants in small flower-beds and in window boxes. This makes it easier to sow seeds or plant seedlings, and to pull up any smaller annual weeds that grow between established plants. The flat fork is best for lifting up bigger weeds, complete with their roots, once you have loosened the ground. Take care when using.

▲ *Flat and angled hand fork*

Gardening scissors

Like normal scissors, gardening scissors can be used for all kinds of tasks in the garden, from cutting string and twine to length and opening seed packets to snipping off dead flower-heads and tidying up straggly plants. They are safer than secateurs (pruners), although they will not cut through thicker twigs or branches in the same way, so you may need to use secateurs sometimes with adult supervision. Take care when using them and never leave them lying open on a surface or the ground. Adult supervision is required.

▲ *Gardening scissors*

Dibber

Used for making a deep hole in which to plant a seedling, or to make drills or furrows (long, shallow grooves) for sowing rows of seeds, a dibber (dibble) is a useful, but not essential, tool. If you don't have one, you can use a thick stick instead. Take care when using.

▶ *Dibber*

Plant labels

It is useful to mark where you've sown seeds or planted bulbs in the border, and sowings in pots and trays should always be labelled with the plant name and date. On bigger labels you could also add notes to yourself saying how often plants need feeding or when to harvest. There are fun labels to buy, or make your own from old lolly (popsicle) sticks or strips of plastic cut from clean yogurt containers.

▲ *Plant labels*

Garden twine

Thicker and softer than normal string, garden twine is used for tying sticks together, for attaching plants to supports or for marking straight lines for sowing. ▲ *Garden twine*

Gloves

Use these to protect your hands from thorns, wood splinters and stinging nettles and to keep them clean when doing a really mucky garden job. Try to find a pair that fits properly – if they are too big they can be difficult to work in. Some types are thicker for thorn protection and others have rubber grips on the palms.

▲ *Gloves*

Bucket

Having a bucket to hand is very useful. They are great for plunging plants to wet the roots before planting, collecting clippings, carrying soil and compost and even for transporting hand tools. There are many sizes, but do not overfill a larger one or it may be too heavy to carry.

▲ *Bucket*

Watering can

An essential piece of equipment for watering and feeding, try to get a can with a handle at the side and the top, since this will help you handle it and put water where it is needed. Ones with a 'rose' or sprinkler fitting on the end are best for watering delicate seedlings and young plants. Take it off to water the base of a plant, under the leaves. Do not overfill or it may be too heavy to carry.

▲ *Watering can*

▶ *Spade*

Spade

Used for digging big holes or for turning over the soil to mix in compost or manure, spades are one of the most useful pieces of equipment. Try to get one that is not too tall for you, or you will find it hard to use. Since the edge of the blade is sharp, you must always wear stout shoes or boots. Adult supervision is required and great care should be taken when using one.

Hoe

A long-handled piece of equipment, a hoe or cultivator is useful for weeding and breaking up the soil surface ready for sowing. It slices like a knife under the roots of weeds, which then shrivel up and die in dry weather and can easily be pulled up. Because the hoe has a long handle, you don't have to bend down to weed, so no backache! Like spades, hoes have a sharp cutting edge, so you must always ask an adult to supervise and take great care when using.

◀ *Standard rake*   ▶ *Hoe*

Rakes

There are two types of rakes: standard soil rakes and spider (leaf) or spring tine rakes. Soil rakes have rigid prongs set at a right angle to the handle. They are used for loosening and levelling out soil. Spring tine rakes have much thinner prongs that fan out from the end of the handle. These are used for gathering leaves or small bits of twig from lawns. Never leave rakes or other long-handled tools lying on the ground. Adult supervision is required.

Wheelbarrow

Extremely useful for transporting tools, compost and plants around the garden, wheelbarrows are available in several sizes. Use one that is the correct size for you, and never overload it. They can be heavy, so adult supervision is required and you may need to ask for help.

▲ *Spider rake*

◀ *Wheelbarrow*

Warning!

Adult supervision is always required when children are using sharp or potentially dangerous implements, such as garden forks. Adult help may also be required for any lifting or moving anything heavy. Children should not use saws, hammers, drills or other electrical garden equipment. It is up to the parent or carer to ensure the child is working safely.

How does your garden grow?

In this chapter you'll find out how plants work, what they need to thrive and why they are so useful to us. You'll be introduced to the way plants are named and what plant parts are called. Budding scientists will enjoy looking at soil and learning about why healthy soil is full of tiny creatures, and there are fascinating facts about nature's cycles, the weather and seasons.

Why we need plants

If it wasn't for the green stuff all around us, we simply wouldn't exist. Plants create the air we breathe (oxygen) as a by-product when they use the sun's energy to convert carbon dioxide into sugars. These sugars form the building blocks right at the start of the food chain.

► *You can grow many plants in all kinds of different containers.*

Nature's favourite colour

Plant leaves and stems contain a green colouring called chlorophyll. This allows plants to trap the sun's energy and use it to split water from the soil into hydrogen and oxygen. The hydrogen combines with carbon dioxide, which the plant takes in through holes in the leaves, and the result is sugar and oxygen. The sugar is used as the plant's energy, while the oxygen is released and we, and other animals, breathe it in.

Seas, lakes and rivers are full of tiny plants, called algae and phytoplankton. These mop up excess carbon dioxide – a potentially harmful greenhouse gas – and stop the earth from becoming too hot.

Food for all

Plants need food to survive. This is created during a process called photosynthesis, when materials are created including cellulose, a plant building block, and starch, a way for plants to store excess sugars.

Everybody benefits from plants, whether they are eaten directly or by animals that we eat. Even water creatures eat phytoplankton and algae, and these are eaten by fish, which end up on the dinner table.

As well as vegetables, there are all kinds of fruits, seeds, grains and nuts that we can eat. And, there's sugar from sugar cane or sugar beet and honey, made by bees from the plant nectar they collect.

Useful plants

Not all plants are edible (some are poisonous!), however we have discovered some that help us feel better if we are ill. Many medicines we use today are based on chemicals made by plants and herbs and you can still buy herbal remedies, teas and infusions.

Plants are grown to provide straw, sedge and rushes, for building thatched roofs or for weaving. Clothes are made from spun cotton, hemp and flax. Trees are cut for timber used to build houses and other structures, and wood pulp makes paper and cardboard. Plants that died millions of years ago and that have turned into coal are burnt to keep us warm or to generate electricity. In the future, plants may be grown to produce biofuels, a renewable energy source used to power cars and machines.

Plants are cool!

Plants help to keep our surroundings cool, especially in towns and cities where concrete, tarmac and brick buildings store and give out a lot of heat. They also act like sponges, absorbing harmful air pollution, soaking up rainfall and helping to prevent flooding. The protective covering supplied by trees and bushes also slows down the wearing away of soil by wind and rain.

Plants make our world more beautiful and colourful. And when they take root, all kinds of creatures move in too. There's a dazzling array of flower colours and forms and two-tone and textured foliage. You get such a feeling of achievement from the plants you have nurtured, the pots and beds you have planted, and the fruits, vegetables and herbs you have grown, picked and eaten.

▲ *The green colour of leaves is due to chlorophyll.*

▲ *Everyone enjoys the fragrance and aroma of plants.*

Plant parts and plant naming

There are lots of types of plants, but however different they look, garden plants usually have a common basic structure, which is useful to understand. It's also a good idea to become familiar with the scientific plant names, which identify each plant precisely.

▶ *If you look closely at plants you will be able to see the different parts.*

The structure of plants

Plants come in a huge range of shapes and sizes. The blanket flower shown below is a typical example of the daisy family. Like most plants it has a **root system**, which supplies the plant with water and nutrients from the soil. These are drawn up the **main stem**, along branches to **leaves** and **flowers**. This species has open-centred blooms but the actual flowers are tiny, without **petals** and are tightly clustered in the central disc. Botanists call these **disc florets**, and the petals **ray florets**. Notice the protective covering of green, leaf-like bracts that encase the flower-buds. These are called **sepals**.

The flowers themselves have male and female parts. Some pollinate themselves, while others need wind or insects to carry the pollen from one flower to another. To attract insects, they often have brightly coloured **petals**. The centre may be marked with a contrasting 'target' that helps insects home in on the nectar and pollen.

When the male pollen grains land on the sticky **stigma** (the female part of the flower), they grow down the style into the seed-bearing **ovary** at the base of the stigma. When this happens, pollination takes place and seeds are produced.

Naming plants

All living things, not just plants, are given a scientific name, mostly based on Latin. The first word of the name is the **genus**. This describes a group of plants that are closely related. The second word refers to the **species**. This identifies all the different plant types that belong in the genus. In many cases there is more than one species in the genus. For example, *Prunus persica* is a peach, while *Prunus avium* is a cherry.

Subtle differences within a species are described by a third word, which tells you what variety, subspecies or form the plant is. If the plant is artificially created, the variation is called a **cultivar**. The variations are written in single quotation marks. A variety of *Prunus persica* is *Prunus persica* 'Bonanza'. Lots of species, such as apples, have many varieties, including names you will recognize, such as 'Granny Smith' or 'Golden Delicious'.

As well as scientific names, many plants also have common names. Some well-known names are 'daisy', 'poppy' or 'lily'. These are fine for talking about plants in general, but common names often vary so you do need to know the scientific names if you want to be more precise. For this reason we have given the scientific names as well as the common names (where there is one) in the plant lists. This means you can buy exactly the right thing.

PARTS OF A PLANT

disc florets
sepals
flower stem
seed-head
flower-bud
leaf
root system
flower
petal (ray floret)
main stem

What is soil?

When you're digging in the dirt or making mud pies, you might not realize how valuable the crumbly brown stuff is. If it wasn't for soil, the earth would be a pretty barren place. Most plants need it to grow into, as few, apart from mosses and lichens, can survive on bare rock.

► *Knowing your soil type lets you look after it better.*

Raw materials

Soil is a mixture of finely ground-up rocks, sand and rotted-down plant and animal remains. There are many different soil types named according to how they were formed and where they come from. Basic types include sand, loam or clay, each of which has different properties.

WHAT'S YOUR SOIL TYPE?

To work out your soil type, go into the garden and see what it looks like and how it feels.

Sandy soils These types are pale and very free-draining because of the high sand content in them. They are easy to weed and warm up quickly in spring, but can dry out easily.

Loam soils These types of soil are dark and crumbly and usually quite fertile. They contain a mixture of clay and sand as well as lots of rotted plant and animal matter.

Clay soils These types of soil are slow to warm up in spring and in winter are often waterlogged. In summer they can sometimes dry hard like concrete, and crack.

Acid or alkaline?

As well as the different soil types, soil can have a different pH. The pH scale runs from 1 to 14, where 1 is extremely acidic and 14 extremely alkaline. The number 7 is the midway or neutral point. Most garden soils have a pH ranging from slightly above or slightly below neutral. On the vegetable patch you may need to add lime before sowing or planting brassicas, for example. Always pH test your soil before trying to adjust the acidity or alkalinity and never apply lime at the same time as fertilizer or manure.

Some plants can only grow on acidic or lime-free soils. These are known as ericaceous plants and include rhododendrons, azaleas, pieris, camellia and many heathers. Others prefer alkaline or neutral soil, so it is important to work out which type you have.

Teeming with life

Healthy, fertile soil is crammed full of tiny creatures! As well as these organisms, which are mostly harmless vegetarians living on decaying vegetable matter, there are fungi and bacteria. These last two groups break down plant and animal remains and produce materials that help bind microscopic particles together and convert hard-to-break-down substances into useful plant foodstuffs. Fungi often have a special relationship with particular plants too, helping their seeds to germinate and their roots to grow properly.

At the next size up, there are the invertebrates, meaning animals that don't have a backbone. These include worms, slugs, ants, fly and beetle larvae, mites, centipedes, woodlice, springtails and fungus gnats. Worms are especially important as they are like mobile factories moving through the soil, pulling dead plant material below and mixing plant foods deeper. As they tunnel, they create channels that allow air and water to get down to where the roots need them. The channels also help soils drain and open up the structure so that plant roots can grow more easily.

What plants need

Light, water and food are essential for survival and growth, but different plants need more or less of them. Fitting the right plant to the right spot in the house or garden and understanding when to water and feed them is part of the skill you will develop as a gardener.

▶ *Potted plants need plenty of water and sunshine to thrive.*

Light of life

Plants need and use light from the sun. Different plants require different amounts of light, however, and if they get too little or too much they can become very unhappy. There are two types of plants: those that love sun and those that like shade.

You can often spot plants that thrive in hot, dry places. The leaves may be thick and fleshy with a waxy coating, storing water inside them. Sometimes the leaves are very small and covered in a flour-like coating, hairs or wool. This reflects the light, keeping the plant cool. Other plants need more moisture and may have large colourful leaves and flowers.

Shade-loving plants often come from woodland areas and tend to be quieter in colouring than sun lovers, with dark green leaves and white, blue, yellow or soft pink flowers more common. Leaves may be large and, with ferns, the blades are often finely cut and lacy. Woodland plants thrive in soils full of decayed leaf and plant material that acts like a sponge, keeping water available. The roots may be fine and fibrous. If you put a shade-loving plant in full sun, the thin leaves tend to scorch or turn yellow.

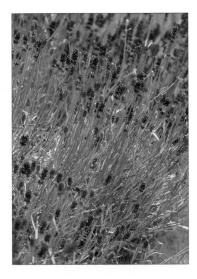

▲ *Sun-loving plants, such as lavender, prefer hot, dry spots.*

▲ *Shade plants tend to need more moisture than others.*

Why plants need water

Water is needed to move minerals and stored food around the plant, as well as keeping the cells, the building blocks of life, the right shape so that they work properly. Evaporation of water from the leaves also helps to keep the plant cool. Water is required right at the start of a plant's life too, to trigger germination, when a seed starts to grow a baby plant.

Overwatered plants, on the other hand, are drowning. When the roots are too wet and haven't got enough air, they begin to die and may have trouble taking up nutrients. Very wet weather can cause this problem outside, and it is common in plants in containers that have been given too much water.

So keep an eye on your plants and feel the soil to see if it is too dry or wet. Wilting leaves are a sign of thirst and if the soil is dry give it a thorough soaking. However, if the soil is damp, something may have attacked or blocked the roots and the plant simply can't drink the water that's there. If you don't tackle a thirsty plant quickly, it may not recover fully.

Signs of overwatering include dropping or drooping leaves and soggy compost (soil mix). You may need to carefully take the plant out of its pot and pat the root-ball with kitchen paper to draw out water, or stand the plant on kitchen paper overnight. Repot the plant, adding extra compost if needed.

How plants drink

The way plants draw up water from the soil is very clever. The action starts in the leaves, which release moisture into the air. The loss of water (**transpiration**) creates a suction through the fine water channels that connect the roots to the leaves and water is drawn up through the stems. This process is called **capillarity**. Wind and heat makes plants transpire through the leaves faster, which means that more water is drawn up and the soil or compost (soil mix) dries out more quickly. In cool or still weather, plants transpire at a slower rate, so plants need less water at their roots.

WAYS TO WATER

There are several ways of watering plants. Potted outdoor ones may need watering at any time of the year.

Misting The air indoors is too dry for some plants. Spray regularly with a hand mister or stand plants on a tray of moist gravel. Don't spray plants with felted leaves, succulents or cacti.

Watering from below Plants with hairy leaves can rot if watered from above. Soak the roots from below by standing in a bowl of tepid water. Water trays of newly sown seed in the same way.

Plunging Always plunge plants in a bucket of water before planting to give them a drenching. Hold the surface of the potting compost (soil mix) under the water and wait for the bubbles to stop.

Directing water Take the rose (sprinkler head) off a watering can to direct the flow under the leaves, where it's needed. Avoid watering overhead as droplets bounce off leaves and are wasted.

Watering with a rose Use a fine rose to water cuttings and seedlings that could be damaged by a strong jet of water. Use a slow sweeping motion, starting away from the pot or tray.

Feed me!

Plants, like us, require food to survive. Plants draw up nutrients from the soil through their roots and circulate them via their stems to leaves, buds and any new growth. So the earth plants stand in must be well fertilized before they are sown or planted to give them a good start in life. They will eventually use up the food, which is why you need to add extra fertilizer, especially during the growing season. Plants in pots or containers need most attention as they have access to only the compost (soil mix) in the pots, and will use up their supplies more quickly.

Not having the right food means that plants start to look poorly – leaves may turn red, purple or yellow and look sickly or leaves and flowers might get smaller and overall growth looks stunted. Correct the problem by applying diluted liquid feed (fertilizer) to moistened soil or compost, following packet instructions. Keeping a close eye on your plants will help you spot problems early on.

Feeding techniques

Food is available as soluble fertilizer, a powder that needs to be mixed with water before applying; liquid feed, which also needs diluting; granular fertilizer, which can be mixed with compost (soil mix) or sprinkled on the surface; and rotted garden compost or manure, which is dug into soil or used as a mulch.

Feed plants during or just before the growing season. Always follow manufacturer's instructions when applying fertilizers and ask a parent to help if you aren't sure. Giving more than the recommended dose can damage plants. Wear gloves and/or wash your hands after handling fertilizers.

▲ A liquid fertilizer needs diluting with water.

▲ A granular fertilizer needs to be worked into the soil.

Nature's natural cycle

A garden is a wonderful place to observe the cycle of life. Whether you like watching the magic of a seed germinating and growing into a plant, or enjoying the changes in the seasons in the garden, there is always something going on outside!

▶ It is fun to germinate seeds and watch them grow into little plantlets.

The story of seeds
The cycle of growth for plants starts with a seed. Some seeds lie dormant until there is enough moisture and warmth to trigger germination. This is when the seed swells and a shoot starts to grow. This will grow up towards the light until it pops up above the earth. The plant should then mature and, in time, will produce its own seeds. Many of these may be lost to wind or eaten by animals, but some find their way into the soil and the process begins again.

Nature's recycling
Nothing is wasted in the natural world. After plants have died down and leaves have fallen, their remains rot down and return to the soil. Here they feed and nurture the next round of growth. A rotten apple is a good example – when it ripens and falls from the tree it might be fed upon by birds and wasps. Soon, microscopic fungi break down the fruit and release substances that butterflies can feed on. Finally, the fungus starts to reproduce. If the apple seeds survive they may germinate and grow into another apple tree.

The cycle of the seasons
In many countries away from the Equator, each season is different These all affect the plants in your garden.
Spring Bulbs are the first flowers to appear, followed by fruit tree blossoms. New leaves appear on deciduous trees. Perennial plants push up and weeds start to grow. Insects and other creatures come out of hibernation. Birds start to sing again and build nests.
Summer Flowers burst into bloom and the vegetable garden produces its first crops. The days get longer and it gets warmer. Baskets and pots must be watered regularly and birdbaths filled as rainfall decreases. Insects multiply and you hear the bees at work as they pollinate your plants.
Autumn Days get shorter. Many plants produce fruits, berries or seed-heads and are eaten by birds and mammals, fattening up for hibernation or to survive the winter. Deciduous tree leaves and shrubs begin to change colour. Leaves drop and herbaceous perennials die down.
Winter Short days, long nights and cold temperatures slow plant growth down. Evergreen plants, hardy flowering shrubs, climbers and early flowering bulbs provide winter blossom. Birdbaths need thawing and birds need feeding.

FROM FLOWER-BUD TO SEED-HEAD
Here you can see how a flower, in this case a viola, transforms from a tightly folded bud to an open bloom ready to be pollinated. After the bee has visited, the flower begins to fade and the seed-head swells. Finally the ripe head bursts, releasing the seed.

THE LIFE CYCLE OF A LEAF
This shows the development of a leaf. It starts with a leaf that has just unfurled from a bud. It continues to grow to full size, then, in autumn, it turns yellow and the shrub reabsorbs all useful substances. The brown remains are then broken down by fungi on the ground.

Flower power

Here you will find how to grow a wide variety of colourful and fragrant blooms to brighten your garden, at the same time giving bees and other beneficial insects a treat. There are quirky containers for growing pretty or scented plants, and as well as patio displays there are mini garden schemes and bed plantings to try.

Pots of bulbs

Providing a splash of colour, spring bulbs put on a fabulous display and look especially good in pots.

you will need

- **crock (clay piece)**, 1
- **pot** (we used a tall pot, which we decorated, but they can be any shape or size you like)
- **gravel**
- **peat-free potting compost** with **added loam (soil mix)**
- **trowel**
- **spring bulbs**, 1 packet (we used grape hyacinth)
- **watering can**

bulbs

plant list

- ✳ **Dwarf daffodil**
  Narcissus 'Tête-à-tête'
- ✳ **Dwarf iris**
  Iris 'Joyce' (Reticulata)
- ✳ **Dwarf tulip**
  Tulipa 'Red Riding Hood'
- ✳ **Early crocus**
  Crocus chrysanthus
- ✳ **Grape hyacinth**
  Muscari armeniacum
- ✳ **Siberian squill**
  Scilla siberica

1 Grape hyacinths and other bulbs like good drainage, so place a piece of crock over the hole in the bottom of a pot to stop it clogging with soil.

2 Cover the crock with a layer of gravel, then half-fill the pot with compost, using a trowel.

3 Space out about 12 little grape hyacinth bulbs evenly on the surface of the compost, as shown, with the pointed ends facing upwards.

4 Other bulbs may be larger and require more space; follow instructions on the packet.

5 Cover the bulbs with more compost, nearly filling the pot to the top. Firm the top of the compost lightly with your fingers.

6 Water well and leave to grow in a sheltered spot outdoors. Don't allow the compost to dry out through the winter.

FACT FILE
GRAPE HYACINTHS

▶ With intense blue flowers and a sweet, musky scent, grape hyacinths are a good source of nectar for insects coming out of hibernation.

muscari

(!) = Watch out! Sharp or dangerous tool in use. = Watch out! Adult help is needed.

Baby busy Lizzies

In early spring you can buy special little seedlings and rooted cuttings, often called 'plugs', that are cheaper than normal-sized bedding plants.

you will need
- **plastic trug** or **container**
- **utility knife** (for adult use only)
- **crock (clay piece)**
- **gravel**
- **trowel**
- **peat-free potting compost** with **added loam (soil mix)**
- **busy Lizzie (*Impatiens*) plug plants**, 2 small packs
- **watering can**

TOP TIP
▶ You can use these plants to get a head start if you have a light, frost-free spot, such as a conservatory (sunroom) or greenhouse. They will grow quickly under cover.

7 Keep the trug in a warm, light place until there is no more risk of frost.

8 From late spring, ask an adult to put the trug out for increasing amounts of time during the day, bringing it in at night.

1 Ask an adult to cut a hole in the base of the trug or container using a utility knife. Next, cover the hole with a crock. Add gravel, using a trowel.

2 Fill the plastic trug or container almost to the top with compost, leaving a small gap.

3 When you are ready to plant, carefully remove the plug plants from the gel-filled container.

4 Gently separate the plug plants by pulling them apart from each other very carefully with your hands. Try not to break the delicate little roots.

5 Space out the plugs and begin planting them about 12cm/4in apart. You can scoop out the compost using your fingers.

6 Lightly firm the compost around the plugs, making sure the surface is level. Water using a can with a fine rose (sprinkler) attachment.

watering can, gloves and trowel

Flower friends

Some common plant names include a person's name and and it's fun to collect a quirky group of 'friends' together. You could even make name tags to put in their pots, if you like.

you will need
- trowel
- gravel
- colourful glazed pots, 3
- peat-free potting compost with added loam (soil mix)
- plants with people's names (see Plant List)
- split cane (stake),, protector
- watering can

compost

gravel

plant list
* **Black-eyed Susan**
  Thunbergia alata Suzie hybrids
* **Busy Lizzie**
  Impatiens New Guinea hybrids
* **Creeping Jenny**
  Lysimachia nummularia
* **Flaming Katy**
  Kalanchoe blossfeldiana
* **Jacob's ladder**
  Polemonium
* **Sweet William**
  Dianthus barbatus

1 Using a trowel, put a layer of gravel in the bottom of each of the pots, for drainage.

2 Add enough compost to allow the surface of the root-balls to sit about 2cm (¾in) below the rim of the planter. This makes watering easier.

3 Position the flaming Katy plants. Squeeze a couple of extra plants in for a bold display.

4 Plant the tall, annual climber black-eyed Susan in a separate pot. You can grow this from seed in spring or buy plants to train up canes.

5 Top up the compost in all the pots, working it down the edges.

6 Insert the cane in the pot containing the black-eyed Susan. Check that a suitable cane protector is in place. Water thoroughly and stand in a warm, sheltered spot.

TOP TIP
► These plants can also be grown on a well-lit windowsill or in a conservatory (sunroom). Pinch off fading blooms and use a liquid feed for flowering plants every two weeks. Water flaming Katy sparingly.

(!) = Watch out! Sharp or dangerous tool in use.    = Watch out! Adult help is needed.

Buckets of bells

The plants in this pretty collection are all members of the same family. To highlight this and to make the most of the blue flowers, plant them up in contrasting yellow and orange buckets.

you will need

- **bellflower plants** (*see* Plant List)
- **bucket** of water
- **colourful metal buckets**, 3
- **15cm/6in nail**, 1
- **hammer**
- **trowel**
- **gravel**
- **peat-free potting compost** with **added loam (soil mix)**
- **bamboo canes (stakes)**, 3
- **soft garden twine**
- **watering can**
- **liquid flowering plant food**

plant list

✳ **Italian bellflower**
Campanula isophylla 'Stella Blue'

✳ **Milky bellflower**
Campanula lactiflora

✳ **Trailing bellflower**
Campanula poscharskyana

campanula

1 Soak the plants in a bucket of water until the bubbles stop rising.

2 Ask an adult to help you make drainage holes in the buckets by turning them upside down, positioning the nail and tapping it with a hammer until it pierces the metal.

3 Using a trowel, add a layer of gravel to cover the drainage holes and help water to escape, then part-fill the bucket with potting compost.

4 Ease the pots from the root-balls of the plants. Put the campanula (the tall one) into the large bucket.

5 Fill round the edges of the root-ball with more compost, leaving a gap below the rim of the bucket to allow for watering. Firm the compost lightly with your fingers.

6 Add a wigwam (tepee) of bamboo canes secured together at the top.

7 Gently tie soft garden twine around the wigwam and the plant to support the tall bellflower stems.

8 Plant up the other little buckets in the same way and water all of them. Stand in a cool, well-lit spot. Deadhead and feed and water regularly.

Super sweet peas

Sweet peas are hardy annual climbers that flower all summer long. Some grow very tall and are best planted out in borders but it's easy to find room for shorter types on the patio. There are even mini sweet peas that can be grown in hanging baskets! Though often sold in packets of single colours, mixtures usually give it a tryod range of shades – mostly pastels with some darker and more vivid colours. Make sure your variety is recommended for fragrance!

you will need

- scissors
- **kitchen paper roll centres**, cut in half by an adult
- **seed tray**
- **seed** and **cutting compost (soil mix)**
- **recycled plastic container**, 1, cut in half by an adult
- **sweet pea** (*Lathyrus odoratus*) **seeds**, compact variety with an ultimate height of 90–120cm/3–4ft
- **recycled plant label**
- **watering can** with a **fine rose (sprinkler head) attachment**
- **clear film (plastic wrap)**
- **barrel** or **tub**, with drainage holes
- **gravel**
- **peat-free potting compost** with **added loam (soil mix)**
- **trowel**
- **1.8m/6ft bamboo canes (stakes)**, 5
- **garden twine**
- **training wire** or **twine**

FACT FILE

HEAVYWEIGHT BEES

Sweet peas and other members of the pea and bean family have a characteristic flower shape. The upright part of the flower is called the standard and the lower part, the keel. Being big and heavy, bumble-bees find it relatively easy to force the bloom open to reach the pollen and nectar.

bumble-bee

sweet peas

1 Snip the ends of kitchen roll centres a few times, with adult supervision. Bend the flaps in to make bases. Position in a seed tray, then use a container cut in half to pour compost into the tubes.

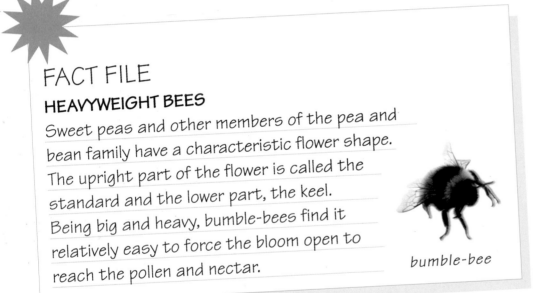

2 Firm the compost lightly with your fingers. To sow, simply push a seed 1cm/½in deep into each of the tubes with your finger and re-cover the hole with compost.

3 To remember exactly what type of sweet pea you have sowed, you could add a hand-made plant label recycled from a plastic container (*see page 124*).

4 Water the tubes in the seed tray using a watering can with a fine rose. Stretch clear film over the pots and tray to act like a mini greenhouse and place on a cool windowsill.

(!) = Watch out! Sharp or dangerous tool in use. = Watch out! Adult help is needed.

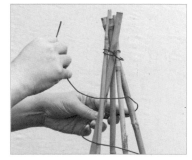

5 Remove the clear film when the seedlings appear. When each plantlet has two to three leaves, pinch out the growing tip with your thumb and index finger to encourage bushy growth.

6 Prepare a barrel or tub by covering the drainage holes with 10cm/4in gravel and filling with compost. After hardening off plantlets (see page 13), plant, spacing up to 15cm/6in apart.

7 Add five bamboo canes spaced equally and tied at the top to make a wigwam. You will need to guide the young stems and climbing tendrils to the supports to begin with.

8 For extra support, tie a piece of training wire to the base of one of the canes then wind it up and round like a coiled spring. Tie off at the top by winding round several times.

Succulents in a strawberry planter

Traditional strawberry planters made from terracotta are ideal for growing your very own curious collection of succulents (fleshy plants, often evergreen, that store water in their leaves) and other drought-resistant types, including many different alpines.

you will need

- **terracotta strawberry pot**
- **crock (clay piec)**
- **loam-based potting compost (soil mix)**
- **horticultural grit**
- **trowel**
- **succulents**, 9 (or enough to fill all the planting holes)
- **watering can**
- **decorative grit** or **fine gravel**

plant list

- ❋ **Cobweb houseleek**
  Sempervivum arachnoideum
- ❋ **Common stonecrop**
  Sedum acre
- ❋ **Echeveria**
  Echeveria secunda var. *glauca* *
- ❋ **Houseleek**
  Sempervivum 'Commander Hay';
  S. tectorum
- ❋ **Purple broadleaf stonecrop**
  Sedum spathulifolium 'Purpureum'
- ❋ **Stonecrop**
  Sedum spathulifolium 'Cape Blanco'
- ❋ **White stonecrop**
  Sedum album 'Coral Carpet'

* keep frost free

FACT FILE

HENS AND CHICKS

Houseleeks (*Sempervivum*) are very easy to grow and can stay in the same pot for years. There are lots of different leaf colours and forms to choose from. Houseleeks are sometimes called hen and chickens because of the way the mother plant produces lots of babies all around it. They need very little soil and can even be planted between tiles on a roof!

houseleeks

1 Bring all your 'ingredients' together so that you have everything to hand when you start planting. Check when you buy that your strawberry planter doesn't have any fine cracks or chips.

2 Cover the drainage hole in the pot with a crock – this could be a piece of broken terracotta pot or tile – to stop the hole from getting clogged up with soil.

3 Mix up a commercially prepared loam-based compost with some horticultural grit (about one-quarter grit to three-quarters soil). Use a trowel to add it to the pot.

4 Fill up to the bottom hole in the strawberry pot with soil. Take the first plant out of its pot and feed the root-ball through from the outside in. The roots mustn't be visible.

 = Watch out! Sharp or dangerous tool in use.   = Watch out! Adult help is needed.

5 Add the other plants on this lowest level, resting the root-balls on the surface of the compost. Next, work more compost around the roots and fill to the next level of holes.

6 Having planted up the middle row of holes in the same way, plant the top row of holes. Firm the compost lightly to keep the plants in place and prevent them falling out.

7 Use a larger, more eye-catching specimen to plant in the top of the strawberry planter. Ask an adult for help to move the pot to its home, then water to settle the soil.

8 Put a decorative layer of grit or fine gravel on the top of the pot around your specimen plant to finish it off and give the planting a sunny, Mediterranean garden feel.

succulents in a strawberry planter   33

Barrel of chocolate

This dark-leaved combination of plants with chocolate in their name has a surprise: the flowers of one plant actually smell of chocolate too! Called chocolate cosmos, this is a tender perennial that grows from a tuber. In a warm, sheltered spot it will flower all summer if you deadhead spent blooms regularly.

you will need

- **wooden barrel**
- **crocks** (clay pieces)
- **trowel**
- **gravel**
- **plants** (see Plant List)
- **bucket** of **water**
- **peat-free potting compost** with **added loam** (soil mix)
- **watering can**

watering can with a fine rose attachment

FACT FILE

CHOCOLATE SCENTS

If you are a real chocoholic you might want to try other chocolate-scented plants besides the cosmos. The yellow-bloomed chocolate daisy (*Berlandiera lyrata*) is the chocolatiest of them all. The scent is released at night but you can still smell it in the morning. Rub the leaves of the chocolate mint (*Mentha* X *piperita* f. *citrata* 'Chocolate') for a delicious aroma of chocolate peppermint creams!

chocolate-scented cosmos

plant list

- ❋ **3 chocolate cosmos**
  Cosmos atrosanguineus
- ❋ **1 coral flower**
  Heuchera 'Chocolate Ruffles'
- ❋ **1 white snakeroot**
  Eupatorium rugosum 'Chocolate'

Heuchera 'Chocolate Ruffles'

1 Cover the drainage holes in the wooden barrel with crocks, then use a trowel to add 8–10cm/3–4in gravel.

2 Plunge the plants in a bucket of water and wait for the bubbles to stop.

3 Pour in a couple of buckets of compost to three-quarters fill it. You'll need quite a lot of compost for this large container. Ask an adult to help you if necessary as the bucket will be heavy. Leave enough room to plant.

4 As this wooden barrel planter will eventually stand against a wall, the tallest plant, the snakeroot, needs to go in first, towards the back. Make sure the surface of the root-ball is about 2.5cm/1in below the rim of the barrel.

5 Plant the chocolate cosmos. They will make more of a show if they are quite close together.

6 Add the other plants, making sure you fill in between the roots with compost as you go.

⚠ = Watch out! Sharp or dangerous tool in use.   = Watch out! Adult help is needed.

7 Plant the frilly leaved heuchera in the remaining space. All the plants in the barrel should be planted at the same level below the rim as the snakeroot. This allows water to pool on the surface of the compost, then soak in.

8 Carefully feel under the plant's leaves with your fingers to check where the gaps are and then add more compost as necessary, working it in between and around the plants. Firm the compost lightly with your hand.

9 Water the plants thoroughly so that the compost is nice and moist. Watering also helps to wash compost into any gaps that you have missed, so you may need to check and add some more compost later.

10 Allow the barrel to drain, then ask an adult to help you move it into position on a patio or some other sunny spot in the garden.

11 Keep your eyes open for slug and snail damage. Water frequently in dry weather.

wooden barrel

barrel of chocolate

Black and white garden

This chequerboard arrangement is created using plants with black blooms or leaves contrasted with white flowers, white-variegated or silver foliage. As only one type of plant is used in each of the containers, you can move them around to create different patterns. To continue the display, think about swapping some of the summer plants for spring bulbs and winter bedding in autumn.

you will need
- **black** or **grey square plastic planters**, 9
- **gravel**, 1 bag
- **peat-free compost** with **added loam** (soil mix)
- **trowel**
- **bedding** and **perennial flowers** and **foliage plants** (*see Plant List*)
- **white pebbles**, 1 bag
- **black pebbles**, 1 bag
- **watering can**

plant list
- ✳ **1 cabbage palm**
  Cordyline australis Purpurea Group
- ✳ **1 calla lily**
  Zantedeschia 'Captain Palermo'
- ✳ **8–12 cinerarias**
  Senecio cineraria
- ✳ **1 coral flower**
  Heuchera 'Obsidian'
- ✳ **2 dwarf Shasta daisies**
  Leucanthemum X *superbum* 'Snow Lady'
- ✳ **3 Moroccan daisies**
  Rhodanthemum 'African Eyes'
- ✳ **3 pincushion flowers**
  Scabiosa atropurpurea 'Chile Black'
- ✳ **2 sisyrinchiums, yellow eyed grasses**
  Sisyrinchium striatum 'Aunt May'
- ✳ **3 violas**
  Viola 'Black Velvet'

FACT FILE

BLACK FLOWERS
So-called black plants have flowers or leaves of very dark maroon-purple. Because they are quite rare, black plants can become collector's items and they are considered the height of gardening fashion! One of the best black-flowered bulbs for spring is *Tulipa* 'Queen of Night'. And from seed, try *Pennisetum glaucum* 'Purple Majesty', a black grass commonly called millet. Birds love eating the seed-heads!

pincushion flower

1 Ensure the drainage holes in the pots are punched through properly. Ask an adult to help fill with 8cm/3in of gravel. Depending on the size of plant, part-fill with compost.

2 Take a viola out of its pot by tapping it smartly on the base to release the roots then tipping it into your other hand. Don't pull the plant by its neck!

3 Plant three violas together in a single container to create a good display. With larger plants you may need only one plant. The plants should not be squashed.

4 Gently lift up the stems and foliage of the violas so that you can see and feel where the gaps are and add compost to fill as necessary. Never bury leaves under compost.

⚠ = Watch out! Sharp or dangerous tool in use. = Watch out! Adult help is needed.

5 Firm the compost lightly with your hands. Ensure that the surface of the root-ball is about 2cm/1in below the rim of the container to allow space for water to pool and soak in.

6 It can be tricky to get bedding plants out of polystyrene (Styrofoam) trays. Push your thumb into the hole below to ease out the plant – in this case cineraria. You can also use a pencil.

7 To strengthen this stylish colour scheme, arrange small groups of alternating black and white pebbles to make a border that goes all the way round the pots.

8 The black-flowered calla lily is the star of this arrangement and is positioned in the centre of the block. To make it stand out even more, cover the soil surface with white pebbles.

black and white garden 37

Spell your name in flowers!

If you have a patch of empty ground, you may have room to spell out your name in flowers. Make the letters big so that the shapes stand out clearly. Choose bushy, upright bedding plants – ones that spread too far will spoil the shape of the letters. It can take a lot of plants, especially if your name is long, so for a cheaper option, sow seed of compact hardy annual flowers.

you will need
- **border fork**
- **rake**
- **slow-release fertilizer granules**
- **bamboo cane (stick)**
- **trowel**
- **coloured horticultural grit** or **washed sand**
- **dwarf chrysanthemums** or **other bedding plants** (*see* Plant List), 40
- **bucket** of **water**
- **watering can** with a **fine rose (sprinkler head) attachment**

TOP TIP
▶ To sow your name, rather than using already-sprouted plantlets, carry out Steps 1 and 2. Then pour some hardy annual seeds into the palm of your hand and, taking small pinches of seed, thinly sow along the line of the lettering. Continue until all the letters have been sown, and then use horticultural grit to lightly cover the seeds. Water with a watering can fitted with a fine rose attachment. Try sweet alyssum (*Lobularia maritima* 'Snow Crystals') or candytuft (*Iberis umbellata*). They will take about 8 weeks to grow.

plant list
✳ **Ageratum**
 Ageratum 'Blue Danube'
✳ **Compact container and bedding petunias**
 Petunia (multiflora types)
✳ **Dwarf chrysanthemum**
 Chrysanthemum paludosum 'Snowland'
✳ **Dwarf tobacco plant**
 Nicotiana Merlin Series
✳ **Fibrous-rooted begonia**
 Begonia semperflorens
✳ **French marigold**
 Tagetes patula
✳ **Sweet alyssum**
 Lobularia maritima 'Snow Crystals'

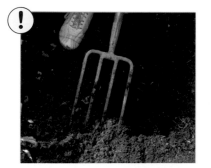

1 Fork over the area to be planted. Level and rake in some slow-release fertilizer (following the instructions on the packet). Adult supervision is required. Mark out your name with a bamboo cane.

2 Use a trowel to make the markings for the letters wider and deeper. If you are not happy with the shape and size of the name, you can just rake over the markings and start again.

3 To make the letters stand out even more clearly, carefully trickle pale-coloured horticultural grit or washed sand along the grooves. Use your hands or fill a plastic bottle and pour.

4 Plunge the bedding plants in a bucket of water until the bubbles stop. You may need to hold them under the water if they are quite dry and floating. Set out enough plants to cover one letter.

(!) = Watch out! Sharp or dangerous tool in use. (○) = Watch out! Adult help is needed.

5 Dig holes for each of the plants with a trowel. As the ground has been forked over this should be quite easy to do. Plant the soaked plants in the holes and firm in lightly with your hands.

6 Continue to plant the remaining letters or your name, spacing the flowers out to allow a little room for growth but making sure that you can still clearly see the shape of the letter.

7 Water the whole name with a watering can fitted with a fine rose attachment. This will help to settle the soil round the plant roots. If any roots are showing after watering, add a little more soil.

VARIATION

• A twist on the theme would be to mark the outline of an animal, such as a rabbit, using plastic lawn edging strip and sow inside the margin with grass seed.

spell your name in flowers!

Spiral maze

Make a secret hideaway with this spiral maze of canes and tall flowers. Stepping-stones lead to the centre of the spiral and the prize, a blue glazed ball! You will need adult help to make it, as the paving slabs are heavy, but once it is in position you can sit back and watch it grow! Change the plants in following years, if you like. Aromatic ground-cover plants, such as creeping thymes, Corsican mint or mind-your-own-business would be good.

you will need

- **tall herbaceous perennial flowers** (*see Plant List*), assorted
- **ground cover plants**, assorted (*see introduction, optional*)
- **bucket of water**
- **border fork**
- **broom handle** or **hoe handle**
- **2.1–2.4m/7–8ft bamboo canes** (**stakes**), 20
- **heavy-duty training wire**, 1 reel
- **30cm/1ft square paving slabs**, 5
- **glazed** or **terracotta ball**
- **iridescent glass** or **acrylic decorations**, 1 bag

hoe

glass decorations

FACT FILE

TALL FLOWERS

Purple top verbenas are perfect for this small maze because they are so light and airy and take up very little room. They also support themselves and flower for months on end in summer and autumn. Mulching with dry chipped bark helps to insulate the roots from frost damage.

purple top verbena

plant list

※ **5 pincushion flowers**
  Scabiosa atropurpurea 'Chile Black'
※ **1 pink hyssop**
  Agastache barberi
※ **10 purple top verbenas/ purple top vervains**
  Verbena bonariensis

1 Soak the plants in a bucket of water until the bubbles stop. Fork over the earth. Mark out a spiral in the area using a broom or hoe handle. Adult supervision is required.

2 Starting from the outside of the spiral, push bamboo canes into the ground, pushing them near their bases. Gradually bring the canes closer together towards the centre.

3 Attach the end of a reel of wire to the first cane, then with someone holding the canes upright, wind around each. To finish, wrap the wire around the cane. Adult help may be required.

4 Set out the purple top verbenas around the outer curve of the maze. Carefully plant between the canes, digging holes for each without disturbing the canes.

(!) = Watch out! Sharp or dangerous tool in use.   (🐾) = Watch out! Adult help is needed.

5 Towards the centre of the spiral, plant the shorter pincushion flowers and finally the pink hyssop or another aromatic plant, like French lavender. Firm in with your hands. Water well.

6 Ask an adult to help you lay out the five small paving slabs in an arc, as shown in the main picture. You could paint on some footsteps (*see* pages 148–9)!

7 All mazes need a surprise at the centre as a reward for finding your way. Here we've used an ball but you might choose some other kind of treasure, such as a terracotta seashell.

8 Define the curling shape at the centre of the spiral by laying out a row of glass or acrylic decorations or some white pebbles. You could also suspend wind dancers from the wire.

spiral maze

Fork to fork

You'll be amazed at how many different kinds of tasty herbs, sweet and juicy fruits and fresh vegetables you can grow even if you don't have any beds or borders. Lots of crops can be raised in pots, troughs and hanging baskets. This chapter is all about using your garden fork to make food for your table fork!

Tumbling tomatoes

Trailing bush tomatoes make attractive basket plants and don't look out of place on the patio. You won't be able to resist eating the sweet, cherry-like fruits!

you will need

- plastic-lined 35cm/14in hanging basket
- heavy pot
- scissors
- peat-free potting compost (soil mix), for flowering hanging baskets
- trowel
- water-retaining gel crystals (see Top Tip)
- dwarf bush tomato plants (see Plant List), 3–4
- bucket of water
- watering can
- liquid tomato food

cherry tomatoes

plant list

✳ **Trailing bush varieties of tomato (*Lycopersicon esculentum*):**
'Garden Pearl'
'Tumbler'
'Tumbling Tom Red'
'Tumbling Tom Yellow'
'Yellow Pygmy'

TOP TIP

▶ To keep compost evenly moist between waterings, try using water-retaining gel crystals. Add water as per instructions. Mix into the compost before planting.

1 Stand the basket in a pot to stop it rolling around. Snip two or three holes in the liner about one-third of the way up using scissors. Adult supervision is required.

2 Part-fill with compost using a trowel. Add pre-soaked water-retaining gel crystals, if you like.

3 Soak the tomato plants (this variety is 'Tumbler') by plunging them in a bucket of water until the bubbles stop.

4 Put the first tomato plant in the prepared basket, angling it so that it hangs over the edge of the basket slightly.

5 Plant the remaining tomatoes and begin filling in between the root-balls with more potting compost. Firm lightly with your fingers. Water well.

6 Leave a gap of about 2.5cm/1in from the rim of the basket to allow the water to pool and soak in.

7 When the plants are hardened off (*see* page 13), ask an adult to hang up the basket in a sunny position.

8 Start feeding with tomato food once the first tiny fruits appear.

Swinging strawberries

With pretty flowers and cascades of ripe fruit, this is a must-have project for the productive patio garden! What's more, slugs and snails won't reach the fruits first.

you will need

- **plastic-lined 35cm/14in hanging basket**
- **heavy pot**
- **scissors**
- **peat-free potting compost** with **added loam (soil mix)**
- **trowel**
- **slow-releaser fertilizer granules**
- **water-retaining gel crystals** (*see* Top Tip on opposite page)
- **2-year-old strawberry plants** for **containers** (*see* Plant List), 3–4
- **bucket** of **water**
- **watering can**
- **liquid tomato food**

plant list

✳ **Container varieties of strawberry (*Fragaria* x *ananassa*):** 'Cambridge Favourite' 'Honeoye' 'Flamenco'

Also see page 242

strawberry plant

1 Stand the basket in a pot to stop it rolling around. Snip two or three holes in the liner about one-third of the way up using scissors. Adult supervision is required.

2 Part-fill the basket with compost that has had some slow-release fertilizer granules added, using a trowel. Add some pre-soaked water-retaining gel crystals, if you like.

3 Soak the strawberry plants by plunging them in a bucket of water until the bubbles stop.

4 Put the first plants in the basket, angling them so that they hang over the edge. Fill round the roots with compost as you go.

5 Continue, using up to five plants in total (put one in the middle). Don't forget you can mix varieties to extend fruiting.

6 Firm in the strawberry plants lightly with your fingers, checking that there aren't any gaps between the root-balls.

7 Water and ask an adult to hang in a sunny spot. Start feeding with tomato fertilizer once the fruits have started to form.

TOP TIP

► Avoid getting leaves, flowers and fruit wet after the initial watering, as this encourages fungal disease. Use a narrow-spouted watering can without a rose to reach under the leaves.

Grow bag garden

Even if you don't have any beds or borders you can still grow many vegetables and herbs in bags. For this project, you'll need a sunny wall. Although you could grow your own plants from seed in early spring, it is much easier to buy plants.

you will need
- **range** of **edible plants**, (*see* Plant List)
- **felt-tipped pen**
- **grow bags** (soil mix bags), 3
- **scissors**
- **bucket** of **water**
- **bamboo canes** (stakes), 9
- **corks** or **cane protectors**, 9
- **garden twine**
- **watering can**
- **liquid plant food**, for edible plants

plant list
- ✳ **3 cherry tomato plants**
  Lycopersicon esculentum 'Gardener's Delight' or 'Super Sweet 100'
- ✳ **3 aubergine (eggpant) plants (patio variety)**
  Solanum melongena 'Baby Belle', 'Bonica', 'Baby Rosanna' or 'Mohican'
- ✳ **3 basil plants**
  Ocimum basilicum 'Genovese'
- ✳ **3 bell pepper plants (patio variety)**
  Capsicum annuum var. *annuum* (Grossum Group) 'Redskin' or 'Mohawk'
- ✳ **1 tray of French marigolds**
  Tagetes patula

TOP TIP
▶ The compost (soil) in the bags is usually compacted. Ask an adult to help you shake the bags and fluff up the compost to make it easier for the plants to root into it.

TOP TIP
▶ Plants that have already been hardened off are widely available from most garden centres in early summer. If you buy them from a protected glasshouse area, however, you'll need to do the hardening off yourself (see page 13). It takes about two to three weeks. Don't plant outside until after the risk of late frosts has passed.

1 Using one of the larger plants as a template, centre it on a grow bag and draw around the base of the pot with a felt-tipped pen. Repeat to make three evenly spaced circles down the middle of each grow bag.

2 With adult supervision, cut out the circles with a pair of scissors. Prepare a planting hole with your hands. Soak the plants by plunging in a bucket of water until the bubbles stop.

3 Plant the tomatoes in one of the grow bags and lightly firm with your fingers. Tomatoes can be prone to whitefly and traditionally marigolds are used to repel these pests.

4 Make a series of small holes along the front of the grow bag with scissors or simply snip 'X' shapes and peel back the plastic. Plant French marigolds in the holes.

5 Plant the aubergines in a different grow bag and lightly firm with your fingers. If you need to make the holes slightly bigger, snip the circle in four places to ease the root-ball in.

6 I like the pungent French marigolds, aromatic basil is another 'companion plant', helping to naturally protect plants from pests. Plant the basil in holes around the edge of one of the grow bags.

7 Plant the peppers in the final grow bag. Insert tall canes propped against the wall for the tomatoes and stick short canes into the compost for the other plants. Top with corks.

8 Loosely tie in the plants to the canes with garden twine as they grow. Water the grow bags daily. Once flowers appear, feed the plants regularly with liquid plant food, following instructions on the bottle.

twine and scissors

Apple and blackberry pie

These tubs will give you enough fruit to make at least one delicious apple and blackberry pie, especially if you grow a dual cooking/eating variety of apple. It'll produce fruit on its own, especially with other trees in the neighbourhood but, like most apples, it has better crops when it is grown near a type flowering at the same time. All those on our list are compatible. Bees will do the cross-pollinating for you!

you will need
- **wooden half-barrels**, 2
- **crocks (clay pieces)**
- **gravel**
- **peat-free potting compost (soil mix)**
- **slow-release fertilizer granules**
- **apple tree** on **dwarfing rootstock** (*see* Plant List), 1, soaked in water
- **thornless blackberry bush** (*see* Plant List), 1, soaked in water
- **watering can**
- **secateurs (pruners)**
- **manure**
- **liquid tomato food**
- **bamboo canes (stakes)**, 5
- **garden twine**
- **pea** and **bean netting**
- **clothes pegs (cothespins)**

FACT FILE
DWARF OR GIANT?
Apples are joined on to different types of roots (rootstocks) in a process called grafting. These rootstocks are numbered according to how vigorous or slow-growing they are. For dwarf apple trees that won't grow much above head height – perfect for patio pots – choose apples on M9 or M27 rootstocks.

dwarf apple tree

plant list
✳ **Varieties of apple** (*Malus domestica*):
  'Discovery'
  'James Grieve'
  'Katy'
  'Sunset'
✳ **Thornless varieties of blackberry** (*Rubus fruticosus*):
  'Helen'
  'Loch Ness'
  'Merton Thornless'
  'Oregon Thornless'

1 Prepare the wooden half-barrels for planting the apple and blackberry plants. Cover the drainage holes with crocks, then ask an adult to help pour in gravel to a depth of about 5cm/2in.

2 Part-fill the tubs with compost, then mix in slow-release fertilizer. Try a plant for depth – the surface of the root-ball should be 5cm/2½in below the rim of the barrel. Firm in and water.

3 Ask an adult to prune container-grown apple trees using secateurs in mid- to late summer to control their height, create an open framework of branches and encourage fruiting 'spurs'.

4 This tree was pruned to create a narrow pyramid. Cut the current season's growth by about half and remaining side branches back to two buds from the bottom of the season's growth.

(!) = Watch out! Sharp or dangerous tool in use.   (✊) = Watch out! Adult help is needed.

5 Cut to just above an outward-facing bud. Adult supervision is required. Keep tubs well watered, mulch with manure in spring and liquid feed every ten days once flowering begins.

6 Modern thornless blackberries are easy to look after, especially those with upright growing stems. Make a bamboo wigwam and tie stems to it with garden twine.

7 Juicy blackberries will be tempting for the birds, so as the crop develops, stretch fine pea and bean netting over the wigwam and secure with pegs for easier picking access.

8 Pick blackberries over two or three days, keeping fruits refrigerated until you have enough for your pie. Apples are ripe if they come away when the stem is gently twisted.

apple and blackberry pie 49

Windowsill salads

Tasty mixed salad leaves are easy to grow on a windowsill even in spring and autumn when home-grown vegetables are in short supply. You can buy packets of ready-mixed salad leaves and cut-and-come-again lettuce, but you can easily invent your own mix using leftover seed. Add zing with mustard or rocket leaves and colourful lettuce, purple basil and beetroot varieties. Cutting leaves and shoots but leaving the roots allows the plants to keep growing.

you will need

- **small window boxes** with **drip tray**, 1–3
- **crocks** (clay pieces)
- **gravel**
- **trowel**
- **peat-free potting compost** (soil mix)
- **slow-release fertilizer granules**
- **watering can** with a **fine rose** (sprinkler head) attachment
- **packets** of **seeds** (see Plant List)

mustard and cress seeds

TOP TIP

► If you have any quick-growing salad (scallion) or bunching onion seeds left over after planting, you can sprinkle a few in with the leafy salad and herb mix to add a subtle onion flavour. The plants don't have to be fully grown before you cut them, so you can harvest them when they are young, at the same time as the quicker-growing salad and herb leaves.

Jen

spring onions

plant list

❋ **Beetroot (beet)**
Beta vulgaris 'Bull's Blood'
❋ **Coriander (for cilantro)**
Coriandrum sativum
❋ **Loose-leaf lettuce varieties**
Lactuca sativa 'Red Salad Bowl'
❋ **Mizuna varieties**
Brassica rapa japonica varieties
❋ **Mustard varieties**
Brassica juncea varieties
❋ **Purple basil**
Ocimum basilicum 'Purple Ruffles'
❋ **Rocket (arugula)**
Eruca vesicaria subsp. *sativa*

1 Set up plastic window boxes with drip trays to keep the windowsill clean. Cover the drainage holes with crocks, then cover the base with a thin layer of gravel using a trowel.

2 Add potting compost, using a trowel. Mix in a small quantity of slow-release fertilizer, following instructions on the packet. The plantlets won't need liquid feeding as they are harvested so quickly.

3 To provide a good base for sowing, firm the compost lightly with your hand. You could also use a piece of wood cut to fit the size of the trough (ask an adult to help).

4 Water the compost using a watering can with a fine rose attachment so that you don't disturb the soil. Preparing the troughs is messy so do it outdoors if you can.

(!) = Watch out! Sharp or dangerous tool in use.   (🧤) = Watch out! Adult help is needed.

5 Decide which mix of seeds you want to grow and, taking just a few seeds of each, sprinkle them evenly over the compost surface. Don't sow too thickly – the plants need room to grow.

6 Cover the seeds lightly with more compost. Place the trough on the windowsill. Keep well watered as the seedlings develop. You'll start to see signs of growth in about a week.

7 When the seedlings are a few centimetres (a few inches) tall, start picking the leaves with your fingers. The variety will have an influence on the taste. Mizuna, rocket, mustard and coriander are more intensely flavoured than other types.

rocket

TOP TIP

▶ For a crunchy salad sow any kind of pea in pots of moist compost about 2½cm/1in deep. Cut the shoots with tendrils when they are 7.5–10cm/3–4in tall.

Herb pyramid

This tiered planting of herbs is a clever way of cramming a lot of plants into a small space. The good drainage created by the arrangement of the pots suits most kitchen herbs. We've mixed in ornamental varieties to liven up the display.

you will need

- **terracotta pots** that **stack inside each other**, 3
- **crocks (clay pieces)**
- **gravel**
- **trowel**
- **bucket** of **water**
- **selection** of **herbs** (*see* Plant List)
- **peat-free potting compost** with **added loam (soil mix)**
- **watering can**

---

plant list

✳ **Chives**
  Allium schoenoprasum
✳ **Common thyme**
  Thymus vulgaris
✳ **Cotton lavender**
  Santolina chamaecyparissus
✳ **Dwarf lavender**
  Lavandula angustifolia 'Hidcote'
✳ **French tarragon**
  Artemisia dracunculus
✳ **Golden marjoram**
  Origanum vulgare 'Aureum'

cotton lavender

✳ **Golden thyme**
  Thymus pulegioides 'Bertram Anderson'
✳ **Parsley**
  Petroselinum crispum
✳ **Pineapple mint**
  Mentha suaveolens 'Variegata'
✳ **Purple sage**
  Salvia officinalis 'Purpurascens'
✳ **Rosemary**
  Rosmarinus officinalis
✳ **Variegated marjoram**
  Origanum vulgare 'Country Cream'

purple sage

1 Cover the drainage hole of the largest pot with a crock and add about 2½cm/1in of gravel using a trowel. Soak the herbs by plunging them in a bucket of water until the bubbles stop.

2 Half-fill the pot with compost and set the next largest pot on top. Add a little more compost into the gap between the pots, then plant the variegated marjoram in the space.

3 In order to fit the herbs' root-balls into the narrow gap more easily, gently squeeze them into an oval shape with your fingers. Plant the golden thyme, filling round the roots with potting mix.

4 Half-fill the middle pot of the tier with compost and position the smallest pot on top. Add more compost to the gap between the second and third pots and plant the purple-leaved culinary sage there.

5 Plant the pot of chives next to the sage. The chives' narrow, grassy leaves make a fine contrast with the sage leaves and the pink chive flowers also work well with the purple foliage.

6 Continue planting up the bottom and middle tiers, adding parsley, pineapple mint and golden marjoram to the base; cotton lavender and common thyme to the middle.

(!) = Watch out! Sharp or dangerous tool in use. (⚒) = Watch out! Adult help is needed.

7 Fill all the gaps between the plants with potting compost and finally fill the top pot. Plant the French tarragon and grey-leaved lavender, leaving room for a small rosemary plant.

8 Plant the rosemary and firm in all the plants, checking for gaps between the root-balls. Water the herb pyramid thoroughly and leave to drain. Position in full sun.

TOP TIP

▶ To be able to keep picking herbs in winter, ask an adult to help you move the pyramid into a greenhouse or cool conservatory (sun room) so that the plants keep growing.

herb pyramid   53

Monster pumpkin pet

Even if you don't manage to grow a giant pumpkin, you'll have fun with this sprawling animal. For a really impressive pumpkin on Hallowe'en, grow one of the big boys, such as 'Atlantic Giant'. But, if you prefer sweet little pumpkins, which are better for eating, try 'Baby Bear'.

you will **need**

- small pots, 3
- peat-free seed and cutting compost (soil mix)
- small dibber or cane (stake)
- pumpkin seeds, 3
- windowsill propagator or plastic bags and sticks
- 13cm/5in pots, 3
- peat-free compost with added loam (soil mix)
- well-rotted manure
- border fork or spade
- trowel
- watering can
- horticultural fleece (floating row cover) or cloches (hot caps)
- wires and canes (stakes)
- tomato food
- tiles or bricks
- secateurs (pruners)

plant list
✱ **Varieties of pumpkin (*Cucurbita pepo*):**
'Atlantic Giant'
'Autumn Gold Improved'
'Hundredweight'
'Jack of All Trades'
'Jack-be-little'
'Baby Bear'

1 Fill three small pots with moist peat-free seed and cutting compost, then make a hole 2.5cm/1in deep with a dibber (dibble) or cane in the middle of each.

2 Sow the seeds on their edges rather than flat. Put the pots in a windowsill propagator, or cover each pot with a sealed plastic bag. Don't exclude light.

3 After the plants have germinated and grown on for a while, move into 13cm/5in pots filled with peat-free compost in a warm, light spot. Prepare the pumpkin patch outside by digging in plenty of manure with a spade or fork.

4 Plant the baby pumpkins after the risk of frost has passed in late spring or early summer. First harden off gradually over a two-week period. Dig holes in the prepared ground with a trowel and plant the pumpkins. Water.

5 Keep an eye on the weather and cover plants with horticultural fleece or large cloches during colder periods. Once the plants start to grow away, guide the stems where you need them to grow.

6 Tendrils help the plant to climb, so provide support in the form of wires and canes. Male flowers appear first on upright stems. Females (shown here) produce baby pumpkins.

FACT FILE
FAMILY AND FRIENDS
The pumpkin is a member of a vegetable family called the Cucurbitaceae. Cucurbits include squashes, courgettes or zucchini, marrows, melons, gourds and cucumbers.

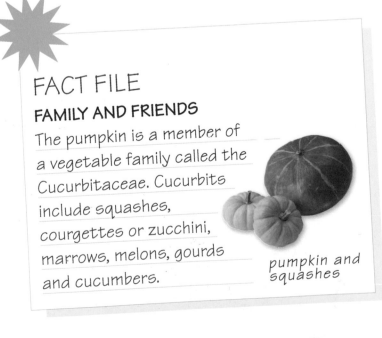

pumpkin and squashes

(!) = Watch out! Sharp or dangerous tool in use.   (🔧) = Watch out! Adult help is needed.

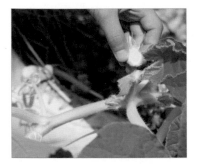

7 Water during dry spells and mulch. Feed with tomato food. Once you can see three pumpkins growing well, pick off the rest to encourage monster fruits.

8 Developing pumpkins should rest on a dry surface, not on the damp earth, otherwise they could rot. Support the fruits with tiles or bricks.

9 If the pumpkin pet is starting to get too big for its boots and is romping over other plants, ask an adult to help you cut some of the stems back with secateurs.

10 To ripen the fruits, cut off any leaves that are shading them. Leave attached to the plant until the skin is really hard.

pumpkin seeds

monster pumpkin pet   **55**

Garden safari

This chapter reveals different ways to discover more about the creatures that share our gardens and how to encourage them to stick around. You can make habitats for all kinds of animal life, both large and small, as well as feeding stations and even places for them to nest or hibernate. So, get planting, and your blooms will soon be buzzing!

Cardboard box hide

You can have hours of fun with this easy-to-make bird hide. Based on a giant cardboard box, some adhesive tape and left-over paints, the project is cheap to make and you'll soon be getting to know the different visitors to your garden. Make yourself comfortable in the hide by sitting it on a thick sheet of plastic to stop damp coming up from the soil and by kneeling on some old cushions.

you will need
- **large cardboard box**
- **chalk**
- **parcel (package) tape**
- **utility knife** (for adult use only)
- **decorating sponge**, cut into pieces
- **paint tray** or **shallow dish**
- **dark green, light green** and **light brown** artist's acrylic paints
- **hanging bird feeders**
- **face paints** (optional)
- **binoculars** (optional)
- **plastic sheeting**

FACT FILE
MUSIC TO YOUR EARS
Birds are particularly active and vocal during the spring and early summer nesting period. They start to sing as the days get longer and only a few birds sing in the winter. You can tell various bird species' call or song even if you can't see them. Listen carefully and you'll soon learn which is which.

starling

TOP TIP
▶ Take a field guide with identification pictures with you into the hide and a pair of binoculars for observing birds in more detail.

binoculars

1 Draw circular, square and rectangular holes in the front of the box using chalk. Remember, when the flaps are closed, some holes will need cutting through two layers, so you need to draw these too.

2 Use parcel tape to strengthen the box and seal up spare flaps for rigidity. Put the box on its side and ask an adult to remove one of the flaps at the back and cut out the holes with a utility knife.

3 Use a piece of chalk to sketch on different leaf shapes to create the camouflage design. Your aim is to make the hide blend in as much as possible with the background, so look closely at the foliage in your garden.

4 Use a piece of decorating sponge to daub on some green paint around the design. Rinse out the sponge and add some pale green paint, then repeat with some light brown. You don't have to be too careful.

(!) = Watch out! Sharp or dangerous tool in use.   (✂) = Watch out! Adult help is needed.

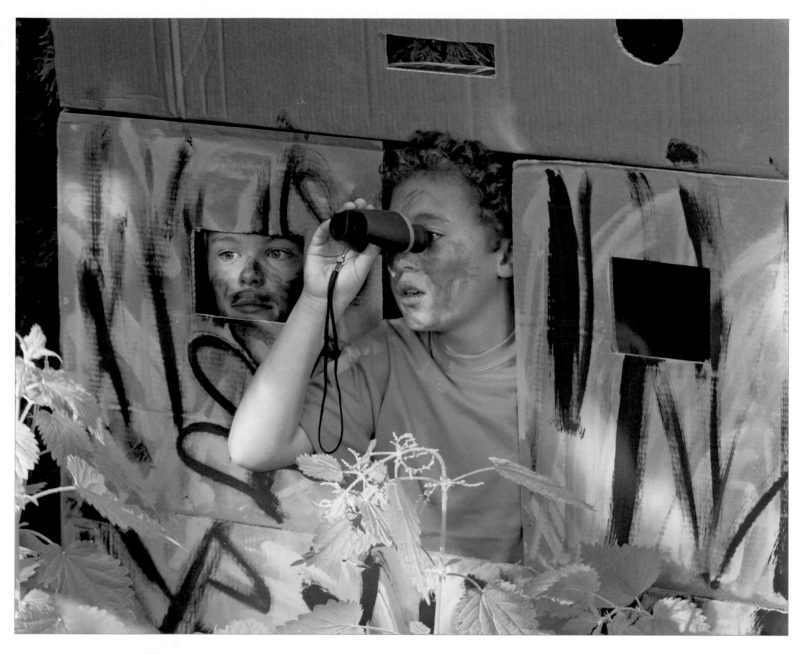

5 Finally, paint on some streaks of black to look like leaf shadows. For camouflage to work, you need both light and dark areas and colours, because these help break up the outline of the hide.

6 Place the hide among greenery or against a similar-looking backdrop to the painted camouflage design. Hang bird feeders in front of the hide at least a week before you start using it.

7 Move slowly and enter the hide from the back. Open or close the main flap to give you different views. Once inside, keep as quiet and still as possible. Green and black face paints will camouflage your features.

8 Be patient! It may be a while before birds and animals come back to the area. Wear dark, dull coloured clothing when you go bird-watching. They won't see you as easily if you blend in.

9 Protect the hide from rain and damp with clear plastic sheeting or store it undercover when it is not in use by removing the tape and folding the box flat. It can then be kept easily in a shed or garage.

Make a bird table

This bird table can be made from any leftover scraps of wood. It can be hung from a tree branch, suspended from a pergola or even hooked over a washing (laundry) line. Swinging high above the ground and in a relatively open position, birds should be safe from cats and can eat to their hearts' content.

you will need

- **2cm/¾in square long piece** of **wood**
- **square piece** of **plywood**
- **pencil**
- **saw** (for adult use only)
- **hammer**
- **long galvanized nails**
- **drill**, with a drill bit (for adult use only)
- **screw eyes**, 6
- **pliers** or **small screwdriver**
- **plastic sheeting**
- **exterior-quality matt varnish**
- **glass jar**
- **old paintbrush**
- **strong rot-proof twine**
- **scissors**

nails. pliers, twine, glass jar of varnish, paintbrush plywood, wood, screw eyes and hammer

TOP TIPS

▶ If the nails are slightly too long and poke through, ask an adult to turn the table upside down and, while resting on a solid surface, knock the protruding nail flat against the wood.

▶ Clean the table regularly. Remove any old, uneaten food after a few days and use a stiff brush to remove debris.

▶ Don't put loose peanuts on the table during the nesting season (spring to midsummer) as there is a risk that parents might try feeding them to nestlings and the babies can choke on them.

▶ Make sure there is food out in early afternoon and first thing in the morning in cold weather. This helps keep birds warm through the night and to warm up quickly again after sunrise.

bird table

1 Divide the square length of wood into four pieces that will fit around the square plywood base. Mark where to cut with a pencil. Ask an adult to saw them and hammer in the nails.

2 Leave a small gap at diagonally opposite corners to allow water to drain from the table. Ask an adult to drill several holes through the plywood base for additional drainage.

3 Ask an adult to make a small hole near each of the four corners using a hammer and nail. These will allow the screw eyes to go into the wood more easily and reduce splitting.

4 Screw in four screw eyes by hand then, if you want to tighten them up more, use a pair of pliers or thread a small screwdriver through and twist. Ask an adult to help.

(!) = Watch out! Sharp or dangerous tool in use.   = Watch out! Adult help is needed.

5 Spread out some plastic sheeting to protect the work surface. Pour a little varnish into a glass jar and then paint all surfaces of the bird table. Allow to dry, then repaint.

6 With adult supervision, cut four lengths of twine long enough to come together above the table and to make a loop for hanging. Attach each to a screw eye with several knots.

7 Bring together the strings and make sure the table hangs level. Allowing enough room for the birds to fly in, knot the strings together. Tie another knot to create a hanging loop.

8 Work a couple of screw eyes into the ends of the edging strip. These can be used for attaching fat snacks or hanging bird treats. Hang up the table and add food.

make a bird table

Hanging bird treats

In cold weather garden birds can keep warm by eating high-energy foods such as this hanging fat, fruit, seed and nut snack. You can also crumble one on a bird table.

you will need
- **suet**, ½ packet
- **pan**
- **wooden spoon**
- **bird seed**
- **fresh peanuts**
- **raisins**
- **aluminium foil**
- **scissors**
- **old plastic plant pot** or **yogurt container**
- **garden twine** or **string**

TOP TIP
► To speed things up, put the filled container into a plastic bag and place it into the freezer for about 30 minutes so that the melted fat solidifies quickly.

1 Melt the suet in a pan. Stir with a wooden spoon until clear and liquid. Adult supervision is required.

2 Remove the pan from the heat and add bird seed, some broken-up peanuts and a few raisins. Stir. The mixture should be quite stiff. Allow to cool.

3 Cut out a circle of aluminium foil to fit in the base of a pot. Adult supervision is required.

4 Twist a length of garden twine or string to make a thick cord. Make a large knot at one end. This will stop the fat snack falling off the hanger.

5 Holding the knot at the bottom of the pot with the string upright, carefully spoon the fat and seed mixture into the pot and firm it down with the back of the wooden spoon. It should be well compacted.

6 Stand the pot outside to cool and set.

7 When the mixture is hard, remove the snack from its pot and peel off the foil base. Make a loop in the string and hang up.

twine

(!) = Watch out! Sharp or dangerous tool in use. (✊) = Watch out! Adult help is needed.

Butterfly food

Butterflies feed from the sweet nectar of flowers, but in autumn they also like sugars produced by rotting fruit.

you will need

- **forked twig**
- **plastic water bottle**
- **scissors**
- **drawing (push) pins** or **notice board pins (thumb tacks)**
- **red cloth** or **plastic**
- **overripe banana** or **other fruits**

rotten apple

plant list

- ✳ **Black-eyed Susan**
  Rudbeckia fulgida
- ✳ **Globe thistle**
  Echinops ritro
- ✳ **Goldenrod**
  Solidago varieties
- ✳ **Ice plant, stonecrop**
  Sedum 'Herbstfreude' (syn. 'Autumn Joy')
- ✳ **Joe Pye weed**
  Eupatorium purpurea

- ✳ **Michaelmas daisy**
  Aster frikartii 'Mönch'
- ✳ **Purple coneflower**
  Echinacea purpurea
- ✳ **Purple top verbena/ vervain**
  Verbena bonariensis

purple top verbena

1 Find a reasonably long stick with a few prongs that will support the base of a plastic bottle. The bottle will need to be wedged among the branches.

2 Push the stick into the ground among some late-flowering perennials (see Plant List).

3 Cut off the base of the bottle with a pair of scissors to make a shallow container. You may need to ask an adult to help you.

4 Wedge the container into the branched stick. If necessary, attach it more securely with a drawing pin.

5 Ask an adult to help you cut some ribbons of red cloth or red plastic with a pair of scissors. They should be about 2.5cm/1in thick and 10cm/4in long.

6 Butterflies love red! Attach ribbons to the tops of the cut branches using drawing pins.

7 Fill the container with pieces of overripe banana or rotten fruit. You can also buy a nectar substitute, which has to be diluted and soaked in cotton wool balls.

8 Retreat to a safe distance and wait for the butterflies to arrive!

Butterfly pots

Even a small collection of flower-filled pots will attract butterflies, especially if you plant them with their favourite plants, such as the well-named butterfly bush.

you will need

- **assorted plants** (*see Plant list*)
- **bucket of water**
- **assorted pots**, 5
- **crocks (clay pieces)** or **pieces of polystyrene (Styrofoam)**
- **gravel**
- **trowel**
- **peat-free potting compost** with **added loam (soil mix)**
- **watering can**
- **kneeler**

plant list

✳ **Black-eyed Susan**
Rudbeckia fulgida var. *sullivantii* 'Goldsturm'
✳ **Butterfly bush**
Buddleja davidii 'Empire Blue'
✳ **Dahlia**
single flowered cv.
✳ **Ice plant, stonecrop**
Sedum 'Herbstfreude' (syn. 'Autumn Joy')
✳ **Joe Pye weed**
Eupatorium purpureum
✳ **Scabious**
Scabiosa caucasica
✳ **Verbena**
Verbena 'Temari Burgundy'

ice plant

1 Plunge your chosen plants in a bucket of water and wait for the bubbles to stop.

2 Prepare the pots by covering the drainage holes with crocks made from pieces of broken pot or pieces of polystyrene.

3 Cover the crocks with a layer of gravel. A large pot like this will need about 5cm/2in for good drainage.

4 Ask an adult to help you tip in enough compost to three-quarters fill the pots, or use a trowel. Try your largest plant in them for size.

5 Position the Joe Pye weed at the back of the pot, then add the black-eyed Susan. These plants flower at the same time and enjoy the same moist conditions, so can be planted together.

6 Fill in around the root-balls with more compost, ensuring there are no gaps. Check that the surface of the compost is about 2½cm/1in below the rim of the pot to allow for watering.

7 Plant the butterfly bush in its pot in the same way. This shrub is fast-growing but won't mind being in a pot for a couple of years. You may find seedlings coming up in paving cracks later on.

8 Continue planting the other pots in the same way. Most of the flowers featured are hardy, but many annuals, such as French marigolds, and tender patio plants, such as this verbena, are great butterfly attractors.

FACT FILE

adult butterfly

BUTTERFLY SENSES

These insects have good eyesight and are attracted to bright colours. To lure them, grow single-flowered annuals and perennials in reds, oranges, pinks, purples and yellows. They smell fragrant flowers, such as heliotrope, candytuft and sweet William, with their antennae, and taste through their feet!

(!) = Watch out! Sharp or dangerous tool in use.   (🧤) = Watch out! Adult help is needed.

9 Dahlias are some of the biggest show-offs in summer and autumn. Butterflies prefer single varieties with an open centre like the one shown here, which allows them easy access to the nectar.

TOP TIP

▶ Early butterflies need to feed on spring flowers after hibernating. You can help them by growing bulbs and rockery plants including grape hyacinth, crocus, aubrieta, heathers and yellow alyssum as well as honesty, forget-me-nots and early blooming wild or hedge flowers.

butterfly on heather

Bumble-bee beds

An old buried teapot offers a gentle bumble-bee a home where she can raise her young female worker bees and later male drones and young queens in safety.

you will need
- **old teapot**
- **cotton wool balls, kapok** or **soft dried moss**
- **trowel**
- **silicone sealant**
- **bulbs** (see Plant List)
- **logs** and **dried leaves**

bumble-bee

crocus

grape hyacinth

plant list
* **Crocus**
  Crocus chrysanthus varieties
* **Dead nettle**
  Lamium maculatum 'White Nancy'
* **Glory of the snow**
  Chionodoxa luciliae
* **Grape hyacinth**
  Muscari armeniacum
* **Lungwort**
  Pulmonaria saccharata
* **Siberian squill**
  Scilla sibirica
* **Viola**
  Viola Sorbet Series

1 Choose a teapot with a rough interior so that the bee is able to grip. Ones with a broken spout are ideal as the way in will be wider. Fill the pot loosely with soft bedding material, such as cotton wool balls, kapok stuffing or dry mosses, and replace the lid.

2 Find a sheltered spot – under a hedge, where the ground is slightly banked is ideal. Dig a hole for the teapot with a trowel.

3 Seal the lid with sealant. Bury the pot, covering the lid but leaving the tip of the spout protruding.

4 Plant around the spout with early bulbs and perennials so that the queen has plenty of food close by.

5 Arrange the logs to shelter the spout from rain and scatter leaf litter to cover the ground planted with bulbs.

FACT FILE
SLEEPY QUEENS
Bumble-bee queens hibernate over winter and in early spring search for a nest site, such as gaps under stones, under untidy hedges or in abandoned burrows.

 = Watch out! Sharp or dangerous tool in use. = Watch out! Adult help is needed.

Lacewing lodge

Along with ladybirds (ladybirds), lacewings are a gardener's friend. Some green lacewing adults overwinter in bark crevices and our 'hotel' mimics that hideaway.

you will need
- large plastic bottle
- scissors
- corrugated cardboard
- pliers
- heavy-duty, plastic-coated training wire

FACT FILE
 adult lacewing

APHID LIONS

Lacewing adults have transparent, veined wings, bright green or brown bodies and golden eyes. They lay hundreds of eggs and the larvae, nicknamed 'aphid lions', feast on garden pests, such as greenfly, so they are a gardener's friend!

1 Wash out a large plastic bottle and leave it to air dry. It needs to be completely dry. Leave the cap on but carefully cut off the base of the bottle with a pair of scissors. You may find the cutting tricky to start so ask an adult to help you.

2 Roll up some pieces of thin corrugated cardboard, such as the type used for packaging, and push the roll into the base of the bottle. The cardboard should be a snug fit to create plenty of warm spaces for the insects to crawl into.

3 To prevent the cardboard working its way out over time, carefully puncture a hole on either side at the base with the tip of the scissors and feed through some stiff garden wire to act as a barrier. Twist the two ends together so they are secure.

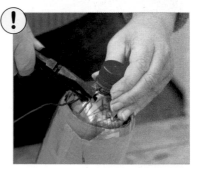

4 To allow the bottle to be hung up outdoors, loop and twist some stiff wire around the neck, under the rim. If necessary tighten the wire by twisting the ends with a pair of pliers. Leave a long piece of wire free to attach to the support.

Wildlife wall

You can build this wildlife wall or habitat stack anywhere in the garden but somewhere close to a wild area, perhaps with a nearby pond or mini meadow, would be ideal. Though you'll need to buy the gabion cages, the contents won't cost you anything if you use all kinds of recycled materials. The name of the game is to create lots of nooks and crannies, some big, some small, to suit a wide range of minibeasts and other creatures.

you will need
- **thick gloves**, 1–2 pairs
- **large gabion cages** (45 x 45cm/18 x 18in), 2
- **small gabion cages** (30 x 30cm/12 x 12in), 3
- **logs**
- **tiles, slates** or **broken paving slabs**
- **bamboo canes** or **hollow twigs**
- **plastic** or **clay drainage pipes**
- **pebbles, cobbles** or **building debris**
- **house bricks**
- **secateurs** or **pruners**
- **pliers**

FACT FILE
CREATURE FEATURE
With a range of different-size 'homes' to move into, all kinds of creatures could take up residence in your wall. Some will relish the cool dampness of the log pile. Others, such as young frogs, toads and mice, will use the wall to hibernate or shelter in. Hunters, such as spiders, ground beetles and centipedes, can find 'dinner' hiding in the crevices, and larger predators will forage around the edges.

field mouse

centipede

1 Wearing gloves, ask an adult to help you arrange the pre-assembled gabion cages side-by-side to create a wall-like effect. Gather together all the materials you have salvaged or scavenged to go into the containers.

2 If space or the position of the wall doesn't allow you to lift the lid right back or prop it open, you'll need someone to hold it while you stack the contents inside the cages. Be careful! House bricks are heavy.

3 Swap over and give each other a turn at filling the gabion cages. Logs make ideal filler material because they offer homes for creatures that bore into the rotting wood as well as for those that shelter between.

4 Tiles such as these old clay roof tiles can be layered in with other materials, such as rubble, bricks and clay drainage pipes, to create a network of spaces of different sizes. Experiment with different combinations.

(!) = Watch out! Sharp or dangerous tool in use. (🐾) = Watch out! Adult help is needed.

5 Loose pebbles or rubble creates another type of habitat or home for minibeasts. Fill the cage right up to the top. If you don't have enough cobbles, fill the centre with bricks, say, and work the cobbles around.

6 Add some hollow sticks including bamboo canes cut into sections (ask an adult to help you cut them up), which will be used by many hibernating insects and may even become nest sites for solitary bees in spring.

7 Carefully lower the lids down on to the filled cages. The spiral fixing acts like a hinge, allowing you to open and close the cage easily. To lock the cage shut, ask an adult to twist in another spiral opposite

TOP TIP
► To assemble gabions, hold two pieces at right angles and twist a spiral through so it catches both sides of the panels. Continue, connecting five sides. Leave the last as a hinged lid.

wildlife wall **69**

Putting up nest boxes

As well as feeding wild garden birds and providing them with fresh drinking and bathing water, you can also support them by giving them somewhere to nest. With a little help from an adult, you could put up several sturdy wooden boxes this autumn ready for the spring nesting season. It can take birds a long time to make their minds up where to nest and they may try out a box by roosting in it over winter before finally deciding whether they want to lay eggs there or not.

you will need
- wooden nest box(es)
- galvanized screw(s)
- screwdriver
- ladder (for use only under adult supervision)
- wire or polypropylene twine
- hosepipe (garden hose)
- nesting material, such as scoured wool or animal hair
- spiral hanging feeder (optional)

wooden nest box

FACT FILE

MARKING TERRITORY

You might think that birds start singing in spring purely because they are happy, but each melody actually carries an important message: 'This patch belongs to me!'. Birds usually choose a number of different vantage points from which to announce their territorial boundaries and the area within is fiercely defended. This is because If too many birds nested in the same spot, there probably wouldn't be enough food for all the nestlings. You might also notice male birds fighting or chasing each other.

wrens mark their territory by singing

1 Walk around your house and garden to find a good site for the nest boxes. Ideally this should be a cool position, such as on a wall or tree facing between north and east, away from prevailing wind and rain. Many garden birds prefer boxes 2–4m/6.6–13.1ft high.

2 Once you have found your site(s), choose which nest boxes you want to buy, depending on what your local birds prefer.

3 Ask an adult to secure the lid with a screw if necessary. Some boxes can be adapted for different birds by swapping the front panel or taking out sections to give wider access.

4 Screw a fixing (fitting) into a tree (ask an adult to help, as you will need a ladder) or loop wire or twine around the trunk, cover it with hosepipe to protect the tree, and attach the box to it.

5 Hang the box on to the fixing. Notice that various box designs have different-sized access holes. This small, round entranceway resembles a hole in a tree trunk.

(!) = Watch out! Sharp or dangerous tool in use. ( ) = Watch out! Adult help is needed.

8 Birds line their nests with soft material. You can help by putting out scoured wool in a spiral bird feeder or hair gathered from grooming animals, such as dogs or cats, which they will take into the nest.

6 For birds that don't mind nesting in and around buildings, such as this shed, ask an adult to screw the fixing under a sheltering overhang out of reach of predators.

7 Hook the box on to the screw fixing. An open-fronted box such as this attracts different birds. Some birds prefer to nest lower down, protected by dense, thorny branches.

9 At the end of the nesting season in late summer, ask an adult to help you clean out the box ready for next year. You may need to unscrew the lid or roof of the box.

TOP TIP
▶ In more exposed sites, such as on the trunk of a tree, tilt the box forward at the top slightly to make it less likely that rain can enter.

Creature comforts

In colder parts of the world many mammals and some amphibians survive the worst of winter by going into a deep sleep called hibernation. This snug shelter can be used for hibernation or just as a place to hide away.

you will need
- **bricks** or **breeze blocks**
- **rigid wooden** or **marine plywood board**
- **hay** or **dry leaves**
- **ground feeder tray** (optional)
- **water bowl** or **bird bath**

FACT FILE

FEEDING STATION
Help small mammals that don't have enough fat reserves to hibernate by feeding them from autumn until spring. Buy specially formulated feeds or contact a wildlife group for information on what to put out. Keep a shallow dish of clean water filled up.

1 Find a really sheltered spot outdoors, such as beneath a hedge or dense shrubbery or between a garden shed and wall. Make a low wall of bricks as wide as the piece of wood.

2 You may need to ask an adult to help you. Check the bricks are level.

3 Next, take a rigid piece of board or wood big enough to create a lean-to shelter and prop it up against the brick wall.

4 Make sure there is enough room for a hedgehog to squeeze under. Adjust the height of the brick wall as necessary.

5 Carefully stuff the space underneath the board with bedding hay, like the type you buy for guinea pigs and rabbits in pet shops. Alternatively, you can use dried leaves that you have gathered in the garden yourself. The board should keep everything dry.

6 Weight down the wooden board with more bricks to stop the wind lifting it or animals dislodging it. Put out some suitable food on a raised stand to help attract animals to the area so they can discover the shelter and perhaps set up home in it, if you are lucky.

(!) = Watch out! Sharp or dangerous tool in use. 🦡 = Watch out! Adult help is needed.

Wild trees from seed

Trees provide vital habitats and food for a wide range of animals, as well as helping the environment. So do your bit and plant a few seeds.

you will need

- **tree seeds** (*see Plant List*)
- **crocks (clay pieces)** or **gravel**
- **small clay** or **plastic pots**
- **loam-based seed compost (soil mix)** or **50:50 compost/leaf mould mix**
- **trowel**
- **watering can** with a **fine rose (sprinkler) attachment**
- **wire mesh**
- **bricks**

acorns

---

plant list

- ✳ **Beech (mast, nuts)**
  Fagus sylvatica
- ✳ **Hazelnuts (cobnuts)**
  Corylus avellana
- ✳ **Horse chestnut seed (conker)**
  Aesculus hippocastanum
- ✳ **Oak seed (acorn)**
  Quercus robur
- ✳ **Sycamore seed (helicopters)**
  Acer spp.

horse chestnut seed

1 Remove the horse chestnut seed or conker from its prickly case. When ripe they should already be cracked open on the ground. Place some crocks or gravel in small pots, then mostly fill them with a 50:50 compost/leaf mould mix using a trowel. Plant the conker in a pot.

2 Cover the seed with 2½cm/1in compost mix, and water. Plant several seeds in individual pots in case some don't germinate.

3 Before sowing acorns, remove the cups and drop the remaining seed into a bowl of water. Discard any that float.

4 Plant in deep pots, about 5m/2in below the soil surface.

5 Put all the pots on the ground outdoors, where they will be open to the elements. Tree and hedge seeds germinate better after alternating periods of cold and warm.

6 Cover the pots with wire mesh weighted down with bricks to stop animals eating them

7 Seedlings appear in spring. Water regularly and pot into larger containers as needed. Plant baby trees as a wild hedge or mini woodland.

Crafty ideas

If you want to decorate your garden and make attractive and useful objects, this chapter is stuffed full of ideas. Most projects can be made indoors or out and use natural or recycled materials, so you won't have to spend much pocket money. Ornamental features add style to the patio and some items are designed for outdoor games.

Recycled plant labels

These brightly coloured plant labels, shaped like the varieties of fruit or vegetables you may be growing, clearly show what seeds you have sown and which plants are which in the garden.

you will need
- **table protector**, such as a plastic sheet
- **plastic containers**, such as milk cartons, yogurt containers or clear plastic lids
- **scissors**
- **felt-tipped pen**
- **artist's acrylic paints**
- **artist's paintbrushes**
- **recycled plastic lid**
- **glass jar** of **water**
- **coloured ice lolly (popsicle) sticks**, **canes (stakes)** or **stiff wire**
- **glue** or **adhesive tape**

TOP TIP
► If you don't have ice lolly sticks to hand, ask an adult to help you split the top of a short piece of cane and wedge the label in, or attach a piece of wire using adhesive tape, which can be pushed into the ground.

1 Cover the surface with a table protector. Cut out a flat piece of plastic from a container with scissors. Use a felt-tipped pen to draw the outline of the shape you want on to it. Cut out the shape. Ask an adult to help you.

2 Paint the label with appropriate-coloured artist's acrylic paint using a paintbrush. Here, we painted a carrot-shaped label orange and green. The paint should be nice and thick; if it is too diluted it won't stick.

3 Other shapes, such as a tomato, sunflower or this pepper, may fit nicely on a circular lid, which you don't then need to cut out. Draw the outline first with a felt-tipped pen and then fill in the shape with paint, as you did for the other labels.

4 Cut pointed ends on the labels so that they can be pushed into the compost (soil) easily. Attach other shapes to ice lolly sticks, canes or wire using glue or adhesive tape.

5 If you like, you can combine the scientific or Latin name, or the plant's common name, with painted decorations.

lolly sticks

(!) = Watch out! Sharp or dangerous tool in use. = Watch out! Adult help is needed.

Cane heads

Garden canes, stakes and sticks are often at head height and can poke you in the eye if you aren't careful. These tops, decorated to look like heads, fit on to the ends of canes and sticks to act as protective coverings.

you will need

- **polystyrene (Styrofoam) balls** or **shapes** (such as hearts)
- **pencil** or **short cane (stake)**
- **surface protector**, such as a plastic sheet
- **flesh-coloured artist's acrylic paint**
- **saucer** or **plastic lid**
- **artist's paintbrush**
- **self-adhesive eyes**
- **felt-tipped pens**
- **raffia** or **wool (yarn)**
- **glue**
- **plastic lids**, such as those from plastic bottles or toothpaste tubes

felt-tipped pens

raffia

TOP TIP

▶ Polystyrene balls and other shapes are available at craft and art shops.

1 Place the polystyrene balls or shapes on a flat surface and push a pencil or cane into the bottom. Adult supervision is required.

2 Cover the surface with a table protector. Turning the pencil or cane, paint the 'head' using flesh-coloured artist's acrylic. Mix up the shade in a saucer or plastic lid if you don't have the right colour or use a suitable paint tester can.

3 Stick on a pair of eyes – and draw on a mouth using red felt-tipped pen.

4 Attach a ring of hair made from pieces of raffia or wool using glue. Wait for this to dry while you work on another head.

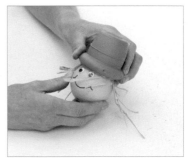

5 To hide the join where you attached on the hair, stick on a coloured plastic bottle lid. Or, draw on hair with felt-tipped pens. When the glue is dry, remove the pencil or cane and position on top of canes in the garden.

Weird and wacky gourds

Grow small ornamental gourds to dry for wacky house decorations. The weirdly shaped fruits have warty, ribbed or spiny skins, often with striped or two-tone green, yellow, orange or white colouring.

you will need
- small pots
- seed and **cutting compost (soil mix)**
- **dibber (dibble)** or **bamboo cane (stake)**
- ornamental gourd seeds
- windowsill propagator
- watering can
- 13cm/5in pots
- **tub** or **barrel**
- crocks (clay pies)
- gravel
- trowel
- enriched potting compost (soil mix)
- slow-release fertilizer granules
- **liquid manure plant feed** and/or **manure mulch**
- **artist's acrylic paints** and/or **varnish** (optional, see Top Tip)

1 Fill small pots with moist peat-free seed and cutting compost, then make a hole about 2.5cm/1in deep with a dibber or cane. Sow the seeds on their edges.

2 Put the pots in a windowsill propagator. The heat provided by an electric propagator is ideal. Don't exclude light. Water occasionally, as needed.

3 Carefully pot on larger plants to 13cm/5in pots when they are large enough to handle.

4 Add crocks to a large tub or barrel with drainage holes, then add gravel using a trowel. Ask an adult to help you fill with enriched peat-free potting compost or add slow-release fertilizer granules.

5 Put the plants in the tub or barrel after the danger from frost or cold nights has passed. Harden off (see page 13) for about 3 weeks.

6 Gourds are fast-growing and spread quickly. Grow up a fence or wall if short of space. Ideally, mulch with manure. Liquid-feed frequently.

TOP TIP
► Harvest ripe gourds in autumn when the stems are dry and have gone brown, before the first frost. Allow them to dry out in a warm place indoors, or spread out on a groundsheet in the sun. When hard, you can paint them or just coat them with clear varnish.

(!) = Watch out! Sharp or dangerous tool in use. = Watch out! Adult help is needed.

Garden signposts

This signpost carries a message for the bumble-bees that simply says 'this way to the flowers'! Prop it up with a stone or brick or, if painting a roof tile, use the holes already in the tile to hang it up.

you will need

- **table protector**, such as a plastic sheet
- **reference picture(s)**
- **paper**
- **chalk**
- **clean, dry slate**, 1 piece, such as a roofing tile, a flat stone or matt surfaced tile
- **white, yellow, black, lilac** and **orange artist's acrylic paints**
- **fine paintbrush**
- **paint palette**
- **glass jar** of **water**
- **clear, matt exterior-quality varnish** (optional, see Top Tip)
- **varnish brush** (optional, see Top Tip)

TOP TIP

▶ Acrylic paint dries to form a waterproof coating so lasts quite a long time outdoors. But, to keep your signposts in tip-top condition for longer, varnish it when dry using a clear, matt exterior-quality product and a varnish brush.

1 Cover the surface with a table protector. Using a picture for reference, sketch a design on paper, then copy it in chalk on to a piece of clean, dry slate.

2 If you make a mistake, simply wipe the slate clean with a damp cloth and start again. Repeat as necessary until you are happy with the picture.

3 Using white paint and a fine paintbrush, go over the chalk lines to make it stand out clearly.

4 When the white paint is dry, colour the insides in sections. Here, we started with the yellow parts of the bee and the centre of the flower. When those were dry, we painted the lilac petals.

5 Acrylic paint dries quite quickly on a warm day. If you put a lot of paint on thickly, it takes longer and the paint may drip, so do thin layers.

6 Don't forget to rinse your paintbrush in between colours and change the glass jar water regularly. Paint on the rest of the design.

7 For a 3-dimensional feel, use darker and lighter shades of the same colours to create shading around the designs. Add wing veins and dotted lines for movement, if you like.

Dogwood stars

You can make use of lovely red-barked dogwoods to make these decorative stars. Hang them up in the house or the garden as a natural decoration.

you will need
- **thin dogwood stems**
- **secateurs** or **pruners**
- **wire** or **twine**, different colours and thicknesses
- **wire cutters**
- **clear, gloss, exterior-grade varnish**
- **paintbrush**

paintbrush

coloured twine

1 Ask an adult to cut some dogwood stems for you using a pair of secateurs or pruners.

2 Shorten the stems so they are the same length, then make six bundles of three or four twigs for each hanging. Lay them in a star shape.

3 Use coloured wire or twine to bind the bundles together where they cross over.

4 Keep tension on the reel of wire or twine and wrap the wire several times around the bundles of sticks before fastening off with a knot.

5 Every point where the stems cross must be wired. Try using different coloured wire or twine for each star, or making the stars in various sizes.

6 The stems lose their sheen after a while, so paint them with varnish using a paintbrush.

TOP TIP
▶ Stars are quite easy to make, but you could also try a simple triangle or a square. Alternatively, make a grid pattern of squares and fill the spaces with hanging ornaments, such as coloured beads.

(!) = Watch out! Sharp or dangerous tool in use. = Watch out! Adult help is needed.

Colourful pots

You could brighten up the patio or deck with painted terracotta pots in lots of different designs and colours! You could also plant the containers with herbs or houseplants for a cheery indoor windowsill display.

you will need

- **table protector**, such as a plastic sheet
- **terracotta pots**
- **glue brush**
- **PVA (white) glue**, diluted
- **emulsion (latex) paint**
- **5cm/2in paintbrush**
- **piece** of **chalk** or a **soft pencil**
- **artist's acrylic paints**
- **artist's brushes**
- **glass jar** of **water**
- **plastic paint palette**

TOP TIP

▶ If you plan to use the pots outdoors, keep the paint looking good for longer by sealing with several coats of clear, matt polyurethane varnish (exterior quality).

1 Cover the surface with a table protector. Using a glue brush, paint the inside and outside of the pots with diluted PVA glue to seal them.

2 When the glue is completely dry, paint the pot with emulsion paint using a paintbrush.

3 Leave the rim unpainted if you like. Allow the paint to dry for about half an hour.

4 Once the paint is dry, use a piece of chalk or a soft pencil to lightly sketch on your design. Here we have used a series of circles.

5 Beginning with one acrylic paint colour and a fine paintbrush, carefully paint in the outer ring. Rinse the brush.

6 Leave to dry, or, to avoid mixing wet colours but continuing to paint, fill in the most central part in another colour, such as yellow.

7 Follow with the darker colour inside the ring (we used dark blue) and finally complete the target design with another inner ring in a vivid shade such as red (used here). Paint different target designs over the rest of the pot, if you like.

8 Another simple design can be made by painting horizontal or vertical stripes.

9 Wait until the paint is dry, then plant up the pot with a plant of your choice.

Mosaic pots

The word 'mosaic' brings to mind Roman villas with their intricately laid floors depicting all kinds of elaborate scenes. But these mosaics designs are very easy and lots of fun to experiment with. Once you've given it a try you'll soon be decorating all kinds of objects around the house and garden! Whatever object you choose though, make sure it's dry first. Why not make some individually painted and decorated pots to give as presents? You could even plant a flower in one.

you will need

- **table protector**, such as a plastic sheet
- **glue brush**
- **recycled plastic lids** or **saucer**
- **terracotta pots**
- **PVA (white) glue**
- **glass** or **acrylic beads**
- **chalk**
- **small glue spreader**
- **exterior-quality, waterproof tile cement**, 1 small tub
- **artist's paintbrush**
- **artist's acrylic paint**
- **water**
- **lightweight, coloured foam squares**
- **small shells**
- **old CDs**, broken into pieces (see Top Tip)

TOP TIP

▶ Ask an adult to break up some unwanted CDs for you by putting them in a bag on the ground and smashing with a hammer. Use wire snippers to break the pieces into the right shape, which can then be stuck on to the pots. Wear safety goggles. The shards of CD are safer than glass to handle but can still be sharp, so take care when using them.

CDs

an assortment of colourful beads and foam squares

1 Cover the surface with a table protector. Using a glue brush, paint the inside and outside of the pots with diluted PVA glue (mix this in plastic lids or a saucer). Leave to dry. This seals the pot.

2 Decide on your design, perhaps experimenting with different shapes and patterns of bead until you find something that appeals. Draw the design on each side of the pot in chalk as a guide for gluing.

3 Begin with the central part of the pattern. Use a small glue spreader to put a small amount of exterior-quality, waterproof tile cement on to the bead. Don't use too much or the excess with ooze out.

4 Press each bead down firmly and wipe off any excess cement with the spreader. Once each side has been completed, finish off with a narrow band of smaller beads spaced evenly around the rim.

(!) = Watch out! Sharp or dangerous tool in use.   = Watch out! Adult help is needed.

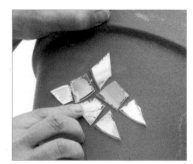

5 For something different, paint a terracotta plant pot with cream artist's acrylic paint. Apply a second coat if necessary and leave to dry. There's no need to seal with PVA as this pot won't be used outdoors.

6 Use PVA glue to stick lightweight, coloured foam squares around the rim of the pot. Mix up the colours to give a bright finish. Wait until the pot is completely dry before moving it or the squares may slide.

7 Another variation on the theme is to again use a painted pot but this time to create a decorative edge with small shells. Attach them in a row or around the rim, using waterproof tile cement.

8 A simple mirrored mosaic design can be made using pieces of broken CDs (*see* Top Tip). Work out your design and draw round it on paper to remind yourself of the position before gluing with PVA.

Mini pebble pictures

These chunky little wall plaques are a fun way to show off your favourite stones and pebbles and, if you want something more colourful, you can add iridescent glass or acrylic beads and marbles too. You can also buy small bags of polished pebbles in black or white as well as more natural shades. These pictures are based on simple flower shapes, but you could make up funny faces, cartoon figures or abstract patterns too.

you will need

- **table protector**, such as a plastic sheet
- **rigid plastic storage containers**, 2
- **clear film (plastic wrap)**
- **ready-mix (premixed) mortar**, 5kg/12lb
- **bucket**
- **trowel**
- **rubber gloves**
- **piece** of **stiff plastic**
- **thin wire**
- **pebbles**
- **marbles**
- **glass** or **acrylic beads**
- **hand sprayer**

rubber gloves

trowel

TOP TIP

▶ The ideal pebbles or beads for this project are ones that are slightly flattened and oval or circular in shape. Instead of putting them in flat-side down, push them in on their edge or narrow end in. This means that the mortar has more pebble or bead to grip on to, making the finished picture secure.

glass beads

1 Cover the surface with a table protector. Line a couple of rigid plastic storage containers with clear film. You could also use recycled plastic packaging, such as margarine tubs.

2 Ask an adult to mix together some ready-mix mortar in a bucket with just a little water, using a trowel. It should be stiff, not sloppy. Wear gloves and don't touch the mortar.

3 Half-fill the lined plastic storage containers with the mortar mix, leaving room for the pebble pieces in the top. Press the mixture down firmly with a stiff piece of plastic.

4 Form a piece of wire into a loop with long ends. Push the ends into the mortar. When the mix hardens this will give you something to hang the pebble mosaic picture with.

(!) = Watch out! Sharp or dangerous tool in use.　(🐾) = Watch out! Adult help is needed.

5 Gather together pebbles, marbles and beads and work out what patterns you want to use in each container. Simple patterns work best. Push in the pieces to at least half their depth.

6 The further the decorations are pressed into the mortar, the less likely they will be to fall out. Spray the finished mosaic with water to clean off any cement dust.

7 Dry flat and leave to harden for 24 hours. Once hard, tip out into your hand; they should fall out easily. Pull off the clear film. Hang the finished mosaics in the house or garden.

TOP TIP
▶ Hang in a protected part of the garden, such as on a house wall. Don't leave them lying flat, or water can collect and freeze, causing damage.

mini pebble pictures   85

Wind dancer

This delicate wind dancer will move in the slightest breeze because it weighs so little. The thin wire frame is almost invisible, which means that the natural elements used – pine cones, shells and feathers – appear to float in mid-air.

you will need
- **pine cones**
- **feathers**
- **shells**, such as abalone
- **pin**
- **nylon fishing line**
- **scissors**
- **wire**

1 Gather all the ingredients together. You may be able to pick up pine cones and feathers on local walks or family hikes through the woods but craft shops also sell a range of natural materials.

2 Each piece will need to be attached to the wire frame. To do this with shells, ask an adult to make a hole with a pin, take a piece of nylon line and pass one end through a hole. Knot firmly and leave a long free end.

3 To attach a pine cone, wrap the nylon line around under the scales and tie off tightly to prevent it slipping. Tie feathers around the 'stalk'. Knot several times to secure.

4 Make a lightweight frame using a reel of wire. The best way to do this is to create a zigzag of wire with a small loop at each 'elbow' or turn. These loops are used to attach the objects.

5 Mix up the different elements for your wind dancer so that you don't have the same things hanging together. Attach a shell to the wire loop with the free end of the nylon line.

6 Attach the small pine cones and feathers in the same way. Don't use heavy items, such as large, closed pine cones or big shells as this will pull the zigzag frame out of balance.

VARIATION
- As an alternative to a wind dancer, you can make a furry spider sitting on its web. Hang it on a wall or suspend from a piece of string.

you will need
- **twigs**, 3
- **coarse parcel string**
- **furry pipe cleaners**
- **pine cone**
- **self-adhesive eyes**

1 Bind the twigs together at the centre with parcel string to create six spokes.

2 Use the same string to make the web. Keep tension on the string as you wrap it around each spoke. Tie off firmly.

3 Make the legs by pushing pipe cleaner pieces through the scales of the pine cone. Stick on a pair of eyes and attach the finished spider to the web with fine wire.

spider wall hanging

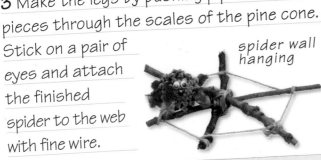

(!) = Watch out! Sharp or dangerous tool in use.   ( ) = Watch out! Adult help is needed.

7 Slowly pick up the structure, arranging the hanging pieces so that they are dangling free from the frame. Gently bend the wire frame into a sort of spiral so that the pieces hang away from each other.

8 You might find it easier to work out the balance of the wind dancer and to thread more pieces on to spare loops if the frame is already hanging up in a temporary position.

9 Once you are happy with the mobile, hang it in its final spot so that the elements can move freely in the breeze. The canopy of a shed or summerhouse, as here, is ideal.

shells

feathers

CD screen

This decorative screen made from bamboo canes and recycled CDs is like a giant outdoor mobile! Use it in the vegetable garden to keep birds off your crops or as a backdrop to flowers. It's amazing how many old or unwanted music or recordable CDs you can collect just by asking adults to save them for your project. When hung outdoors, the surface that isn't printed on catches the light and shows all kinds of rainbow colours, like oil on water.

you will need

- 1.8–2.1m/6–7ft bamboo canes (stakes), 8
- **thick garden wire** or **garden twine**
- **wire cutters** or **scissors**
- **pliers**
- **unwanted CDs**
- **drill**, with fine drill bit (adult use only)
- **nylon fishing line** or **thin, coloured parcel twine**
- **cane toppers**, (see page 125)

garden twine and scissors

FACT FILE

FLOWERING CLIMBERS FROM SEED

Your CD screen can also work as a frame for growing colourful flowering climbers, such as the hardy annual nasturtium and sweet pea. After the last spring frost, sow runner beans directly into the ground, which you have forked over.

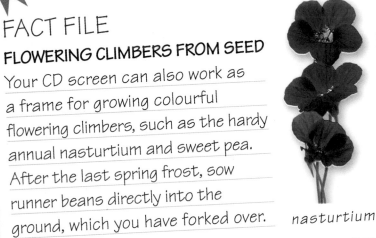

nasturtium

Start Spanish flag and canary creeper seeds in pots on a warm window ledge in early spring following instructions on the packet.

WARNING – Spanish flag seeds are poisonous.

sweet pea

1 Push three pairs of crossing bamboo canes into the ground. Try to make the angles as even as possible. Be careful when moving them into position to keep the ends away from people's eyes.

2 If the ground is very hard, hold the canes close to the bottom so that the cane doesn't snap or bend when you are pushing it in. Ask an adult to help you if you are having difficulty.

3 Join the canes where they cross over with pieces of thick garden wire or twine, cut to length with wire cutters or scissors. Ask an adult to cut the wire. Twist and tighten with pliers.

4 Balance a bamboo cane across the top and attach the three pairs of canes to it to create a series of large diamond shapes and smaller triangles. This is definitely a two-person job!

5 Push in an upright cane at both ends. Attach the top cane to them to create a strong framework. It needs to be able to stand up to strong winds and the weight of climbing plants.

(!) = Watch out! Sharp or dangerous tool in use. (✋) = Watch out! Adult help is needed.

6 Ask an adult to drill small small holes into each of the CDs. Then thread through nylon fishing line or thin, coloured parcel twine, knotting it to prevent it slipping.

7 Use the two long free ends of line to attach each CD to the framework. Position one CD to hang in the middle of each of the small triangular spaces along the top.

8 Hang as many CDs on to the frame as you like. Tie the line shorter or longer so they hang at different levels. It doesn't matter which way the CDs hang. Add cane toppers.

TOP TIP
▶ You can hang all kinds of natural bits and pieces from this screen, provided they are light enough, or even strips of coloured fabric or plastic.

Spooky Jack-o'-lantern

Whether you are planning to surprise visitors at a Hallowe'en party with home-grown Jack-o'-lanterns or just want to join in the seasonal fun of pumpkin carving, this project will give you all the help and advice you'll need. Of course you must ask permission from an adult before you begin and you'll probably need some grown-up help along the way. If you are lucky, your Monster Pumpkin Pet (see page 82) might even produce a fruit that is big enough to carve!

(see page 82)

you will need
- **large pumpkin**
- **medium sharp knife**
- **bowl**
- **felt-tipped pen**
- **small sharp knife**
- **bucket** or **bowl**
- **night light** or **small candle**
- **matches**

bowl   *pumpkin*

TOP TIP

▶ To make a tasty snack from the pumpkin seeds, heat the oven to 180°C/350°F/Gas 4. Scoop out the seeds and rinse in a colander. Spread the clean seeds out thinly on a baking tray so that they roast evenly. Drizzle with olive oil and lightly salt. Roast for about 10 minutes or until light golden brown, shaking occasionally so they brown evenly. You need to keep a close eye on them as they can burn easily. Cool and store in an airtight container. Sprinkle over salads, or eat on their own as a delicious snack.

pumpkin seeds

1 Find a ripe pumpkin and ask an adult to help you cut the 'lid' off the fruit. Leave the stalk as a handle. Take great care with knives and don't use them unless you have permission.

2 Angle the cut so that you can fit the lid back on neatly afterwards. Remove the solid flesh directly beneath the lid. It can be used in soups or to make pumpkin pie!

3 The next step is a bit gross! Pull out all the slimey stuff and pumpkin seeds and put them into a bowl. You will need this later if you want to make a yummy snack (*see* Top Tip).

4 Wash and dry your hands and the knife. Check the skin of the pumpkin is dry, then draw on a face with a felt-tipped pen. Make the features big and simple.

(!) = Watch out! Sharp or dangerous tool in use.   🐾 = Watch out! Adult help is needed.

5 Ask an adult to help you to cut out the eyes, nose and mouth. You might want to use a smaller knife for greater cutting control. Set the pumpkin on a bucket or bowl to steady it.

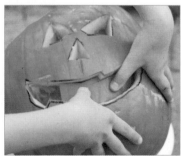

6 Once you have finished cutting, press the segments back into the hollow insides with your thumbs. You might need to do a little bit of neatening up afterwards with the knife.

7 With permission from an adult, light a night light or small candle and pass it through the mouth. Carefully guide it into position with your other hand. Be careful not to burn yourself!

8 Replace the pumpkin lid with the stalk set at a jaunty angle. Once it has gone dark you'll really be able to see the flickering candle, the scary eyes and eerie orange glow.. Spooky!

Friendly scarecrow!

The beauty of this scarecrow is that he is 100 per cent recycled! You shouldn't need to buy any of the materials listed below. They are all things that you can normally find in the house, garage, shed or garden. Do ask permission from an adult first though. Another plus point is that the scarecrow can easily be dismantled and stored under cover for the winter. Use him to brighten up your veg plot – he may even scare off a few crows!

you will need

- **wooden battens (1 x 2s)**, 2
- **nails**
- **hammer**
- **plain pillow cases**, 2
- **stuffing material**, such as plastic bags, bubble-wrap packaging, recycled newspaper etc
- **flesh-coloured acrylic paint**
- **paintbrush**
- **wool (yarn)**
- **scissors**
- **parcel (package) tape**
- **pencil**
- **black marker pen**
- **garden twine**
- **old clothes**, such as a shirt, trousers (pants), scarf, gloves and a hat
- **plastic refuse sacks (garbage bags)**
- **old wellington (rubber) boots**, 1 pair
- **piece** of **wire**
- **fabric flower** (optional)

TOP TIP
▶ Choose whatever theme you like for your scarecrow and even dress him or her up differently during the year or change the hairstyle, for instance, by attaching long woollen plaits (braids). If you can't find wooden battens to nail together, you can make the frame from twigs and tree branches bound together with strong twine.

Hallowe'en scarecrow

wellington boots

1 Find a long piece of wooden batten (head height or taller) and a shorter piece to attach for the shoulders and arms. Ask an adult to help you nail them together using a hammer.

2 Pack a pillowcase with stuffing and gather the material at the back to make a round shape. Paint the face with flesh-coloured acrylic paint. Attach wool for the hair with parcel tape.

3 Draw on the face – big eyes, nose and mouth – with a pencil. Go over with a black marker pen so that you can see the features clearly. Attach the head to the frame with garden twine.

4 Hammer the frame into the ground and begin to dress the scarecrow. Start with an adult's shirt. Fill a large plain pillowcase with plastic stuffing for the body.

(!) = Watch out! Sharp or dangerous tool in use.   🦊 = Watch out! Adult help is needed.

5 Use the top two corners of the pillowcase to tie the body around the neck of the scarecrow. You can hide the join with a scarf. Tie some twine around the middle to shape the waist.

6 Make sausage-shaped stuffing for the arms and legs using refuse sacks filled with newspaper and tied off. Tie off the legs of the trousers and stuff. Stuff the arms, then do up the cuffs.

7 Stuff gloves to make the hands and secure to the ends of the batten. Attach the trousers with twine – the long shirt will hide the join. Put the stuffed legs into a pair of wellies.

8 Add the finishing touches, such as a straw sun hat. Attach with wire to stop it blowing off. You can also give the scarecrow a buttonhole using a fabric flower.

Footstep path

This is a stepping-stone path with a difference – you get to walk in your own footprints! Your left and right feet are used as templates for these brightly coloured designs and the canvas is also most unusual – how often do you get to paint on stone or concrete? Be as creative as you like with the patterns and colours. If the stepping-stones are laid on green grass, bright reds, oranges and vivid pinks will show up particularly well.

you will need
- **paper**, 2 pieces
- **coloured pencils**
- **scissors**
- **stone** or **concrete paving slabs** (30 x 30cm/12 x 12in), 5 or 6
- **acrylic paints**
- **artist's paintbrushes** (assorted)
- **clean water**
- **recycled plastic lids**, 2
- **glass jar** of **water**
- **kitchen paper**

coloured pencils

scissors

acrylic paints

TOP TIPS
▶ Ask an adult to set the stones in position only when they are completely dry, and don't try walking on them for a day or two – wait for the paint to harden. Lay them on the surface of the ground or cut out square shapes to drop the slabs into, making them level with the ground.
▶ Although the paint will last well in the summer months, it needs protection from damp and cold to extend its life. Seal the painted surface with two coats of exterior-quality varnish or a clear sealant.

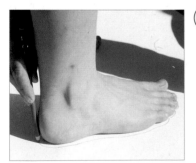

1 Take off your shoes and socks. Stand on a piece of paper and use a coloured pencil to draw around your feet. It's easier to do one at a time on separate sheets. Don't forget the toes!

2 Cut out the footprint to create a template. Adult supervision is required. You can use the same template for both feet. Simply flip over the cut-out to create the template for the other foot.

3 Use the template to transfer the outline to a stone or concrete paving slab using a coloured pencil that shows up well. Slabs usually have a smooth side that's best for painting on.

4 We drew our feet on the diagonal, which looks more interesting. Use a thick, dark acrylic paint and a paintbrush to form the outline of the foot. Dilute the paint slightly if it is too thick.

(!) = Watch out! Sharp or dangerous tool in use.   (🐾) = Watch out! Adult help is needed.

5 Using recycled plastic lids as paint palettes and to keep colours from running into one another. Start to paint your patterns. Make them as fun as you like, though simple designs work best.

6 Fill inside the outline of some feet with solid colour, then, if you like, you can also paint around the outside in a different shade. Give the outline band a fuzzy or smudged edge.

7 Add texture by waiting until the base coat has dried, then using a different colour to apply a pattern. Here we have dots but you could use wavy or straight lines, a criss-cross pattern etc.

VARIATION
• Although feet work well, you could paint any other shapes you like on the stepping stones, such as stars, hearts, arrows or swirls.

Miss Muffet's tuffet

You can have much more fun with a grass dome than the Miss Muffet of nursery rhyme fame did! Use it as a seat or perch, as a high point from which you can survey your realm, as a pitching mound or as sanctuary in a game of tag. Provided your foundations are very well compacted you can build bigger ridges and mounds or even snake-like shapes using inexpensive leftover bricks and similar materials and a covering of topsoil.

you will need
- **thick gloves**
- **bricks**
- **rubble**
- **wheelbarrow**
- **gravel** or **hardcore**, 1–2 tonnes
- **spade**
- **topsoil**, 1 tonne
- **grass seed**, general purpose or hard-wearing mix
- **garden rake**
- **watering can** with a **fine rose attachment**

wheelbarrrow

TOP TIP
▶ When part of a lawn is dug up to make way for a new feature, don't get rid of the turf – turn it into a mound! Put the turf pieces (called 'sods') upside down, packing them together neatly in a series of circles. Gradually build up the mound. Tread it down, cover with soil and use any remaining turf to cover the mound, grass-side up. Water well.

turf sod

heavy-duty gloves

1 Wearing thick gloves, ask an adult to help you lay down a foundation using any spare bricks or concrete building blocks, broken tiles or other building material that won't rot down.

2 Try to arrange the construction under the mound as solidly as possible, leaving few gaps. Next, pour on several wheelbarrow-loads of gravel or hardcore. Hardcore is cheaper.

3 Compact this loose material well. Ask an adult to help you, especially if building larger mounds. Using a spade, add about a tonne of topsoil. It doesn't have to be top-quality.

4 Compact the mound again with your feet. This is the fun part! It must be solid enough for you to stand on without moving. A flat top is more practical than a rounded one.

! = Watch out! Sharp or dangerous tool in use. 🖐 = Watch out! Adult help is needed.

5 Smooth over the mound, using the back of a spade. Adult supervision is required. Avoid using your hands, as in topsoil that hasn't been sieved there are sometimes pieces of glass.

6 Sprinkle the mound with grass seed. This germinates best in mid-spring or early autumn, when the ground is warm and moist, but it will sprout in summer if you keep it watered.

7 Lightly rake over the mound, trying not to disturb the soil too much. This lightly covers the seed, putting it in closer contact with the soil. If patches don't germinate, you can reseed.

8 Pat down with your hands, pressing the seed lightly into the soil. If it doesn't rain in the next couple of days, water carefully. Grass should appear within 5–10 days.

Flower arbour

Arbours are great places to sit and chat to your friends or watch birds or other animals in your garden. They are normally quite expensive, but this one uses a cheap, flat-packed arch set against a fence that acts as the arbour's back wall. With clematis planted on both sides, the arch will soon be covered with lush growth.

you will need
- **flat-pack metal garden arch**
- **small screwdriver**
- **bamboo measuring cane (stake)**
- **clematis cultivars** (see Plant List), 2
- **bucket** of **water**
- **spade**
- **well-rotted garden compost** or **manure**
- **watering can**
- **chipped bark**
- **planks** of **wood**
- **saw** (for adult use only)
- **bricks** or **building blocks**
- **garden twine**
- **scissors**

plant list
✽ ***Clematis viticella* cultivars:**
  'Etoile Violette'
  'Madame Julia Correvon'
  'Prince Charles '
  'Ville de Lyons'

TOP TIP
► Late summer- and autumn-flowering clematis can be pruned hard in late winter to around 30cm/12in from ground level, preferably just above a pair of buds.

clematis

1 You will need adult help to build the arch. Lay out all the pieces on the ground. Follow the instructions to slot the pieces together. Secure screws with a screwdriver. Stand the arch in position.

2 Ask an adult to cut a cane to the width of the arch. Lay the cane down and use it to space the legs correctly. Push the legs into the ground, holding them near their bases.

3 Plunge the clematis plants in turn in a bucket of water. Wait for the bubbles of air to stop. Dig a hole on one side of the arch for the first plant using a spade and try the clematis plant for size.

4 Place a cane across to check the depth. Large flowered clematis are set 5–7cm/2–3in) deeper than the surrounding soil. This helps them recover if they get clematis wilt disease. Others are planted as normal.

5 *Clematis viticella* hybrids are disease-resistant, but to improve the soil, mix a good quantity of well-rotted compost or manure into the soil dug out of the hole.

6 Plant, working the soil well in round the roots. Firm with your hands not with your foot – you don't want to compact the soil as this could affect rooting. Water and mulch with bark.

(!) = Watch out! Sharp or dangerous tool in use.   = Watch out! Adult help is needed.

7 Find some wooden planks to make a seat with. Try them for size and ask an adult to help cut them down if necessary. Make the legs using piles of bricks or building blocks.

8 Clematis climb with twining leaf tendrils and need plenty of support to grow up over the arch. Tie garden twine to the lowest horizontal bar and, keeping it taut, wind around the bars and tie off.

9 Repeat on both sides of the arch. Attach the clematis stems on to the twine. Train the clematis to climb over the arch, tying it in at regular intervals as it grows to provide support.

flower arbour

Living wigloo

This living structure is based on the shape of an igloo but is made from willow – hence the name 'wigloo'! Even before the wigloo is fully grown, you can start to use it as a den. Cover the ground with a waterproof groundsheet and bring in a blanket and some old cushions. Until the walls have knitted together, you can create shade and privacy by draping the willow frame with an old sheet. Make sure you keep the wigloo well watered in the first year.

you will need
- **long-handled pruners**, for adult use only
- **deep bucket** of **water**
- **rope** or **hosepipe** (garden hose)
- **hand shears**
- **secateurs** or **pruners**
- **spade**
- **stout stick** or **stake**, 1
- **rubber mallet** or **lump hammer**
- **watering can**
- **strong garden twine**
- **waterproof groundsheet**, 1
- **outdoor blanket**, 1
- **old cushions**

TOP TIPS
▶ Willow has an amazing ability to root. Keep fresh-cut stems in a deep bucket of water until ready to use. These 'wands' will last many days like this.

▶ In spring, when the buds sprout, remove at least half of the young shoots to allow the roots to develop properly.

WARNING – Don't plant willow near buildings, drains or sewers, as the roots can cause damage.

soaking willow

1 Ask an adult to help you cut some long, unbranched willow wands from a willow tree using long-handled pruners. Put them in a bucket of water until required.

2 Using a piece of rope or hosepipe, mark out a rough circle in a reasonably sunny part of the garden. Ideally the ground should be quite moisture-retentive. Clay soils are ideal.

3 Ask an adult to help you cut down any weeds within the circle with hand shears and secateurs or pruners. Dig a narrow trench all around the edge of the circle using a spade.

4 Use a stout stick or stake to make a series of pilot holes. Knock the stick or stake into the ground using a rubber mallet or lump hammer. You may need adult help.

(!) = Watch out! Sharp or dangerous tool in use.   (🔧) = Watch out! Adult help is needed.

5 Make sure the holes are evenly spaced, 20–30cm/ 8–12in apart. Holding a wand towards the base to stop it bending, push it into the hole. Drive it in as far as it will go. You may need adult help.

6 When these upright willow wands are all in position, move the soil back into the trench, tread in firmly with the weight on your foot and water with a watering can.

7 Starting halfway down, draw two wands across one another and tie with twine. Continue the criss-cross pattern towards the top of the wigloo. Cut off unwanted branches.

8 To make the doorway, check there's enough room for you to crawl through and ask someone to hold the stems together temporarily while you do this. Firmly tie the crossing stems over the doorway.

9 Continue to weave in the side shoots. Eventually, the wigloo will knit together as a solid dome and will just need trimming a few times a year, in winter and late summer.

Weave a fence

This border edging is particularly useful for containing sprawling plants next to a lawn. You can make the fence any length you want – just hammer in more stakes. The plant list shows some of the most suitable plants for cutting and weaving but you can experiment. For the best colour development, cut after or just before leaf fall.

you will need

- 2.5 x 2.5 x 45cm/1 x 1 x 18in wooden stakes
- lump (club) hammer
- secateurs or hand pruners
- plant stems (see Plant List)

plant list

- ✳ **Golden willow**
  Salix alba var. *vitellina*
- ✳ **Hazel**
  Corylus avellana
- ✳ **Orange stemmed dogwood**
  Cornus sanguinea 'Midwinter Fire' or 'Winter Beauty'
- ✳ **Red barked dogwood**
  Cornus alba 'Sibirica'
- ✳ **Scarlet willow**
  Salix alba var. *vitellina* 'Britzensis'
- ✳ **Yellow stemmed dogwood**
  Cornus sericea 'Flaviramea'
- ✳ **Yellow variegated dogwood**
  Cornus alba 'Gouchaultii' or 'Spaethii'
- ✳ **White variegated dogwood**
  Cornus alba 'Elegantissima'

WARNING – Willows and the moisture-loving dogwoods should not be planted near drains or sewers as their roots can block the channels.

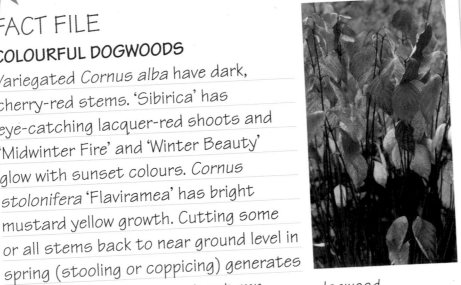

FACT FILE

COLOURFUL DOGWOODS

Variegated *Cornus alba* have dark, cherry-red stems. 'Sibirica' has eye-catching lacquer-red shoots and 'Midwinter Fire' and 'Winter Beauty' glow with sunset colours. *Cornus stolonifera* 'Flaviramea' has bright mustard yellow growth. Cutting some or all stems back to near ground level in spring (stooling or coppicing) generates more colourful stems next autumn.

dogwood

1 Ask an adult to help you drive in a row of equally spaced wooden stakes using a heavy lump hammer. Space them approximately 30–45cm/12–18in apart depending on the length of stems cut.

2 Since secateurs or pruners can be dangerous, ask an adult to help you cut a big bundle of long, straight, flexible stems from trees such as suckering shrubs or coppiced trees. Strip off any leaves.

3 If the branches are forked or have side shoots, ask an adult to cut these off to leave a single unbranched stem. These will be easier to weave in and out of the stakes and won't catch on anything.

4 Collect together bundles of freshly cut stems and take them to where you are making the fence or edging. If you leave cut stems to dry out, they can become brittle, so work with fresh stems.

! = Watch out! Sharp or dangerous tool in use. = Watch out! Adult help is needed.

5 Weave the stems in and out of the stakes, making sure that you work behind and in front of neighbouring stakes and don't miss any out. For the row above, switch to weave the other way round.

6 This is much easier to do with two people, because one can hold the stem in place while the other finishes weaving with it. Overlap the joins when putting in the row above, for extra strength.

7 Press the stems down as you go so that the layers of stems are lying close against each other. Mix as many differently coloured stems as you can find to make the fence look more attractive.

TOP TIP
▶ If you don't have any suitable shrubs to prune, buy dried willow wands from craft or willow weaving companies and soak before use to make them flexible.

Rainy day gardening

When the weather is too cold or wet for gardening outdoors you can still raise a wide range of plants inside to keep your green fingers or thumbs occupied. This chapter even shows how to grow windowsill crops. There are fun 'creatures' to make, bulbs to start off and exotic seeds to germinate and you'll love the indoor gardens and mini landscapes.

Sprouting seeds

It is really, really easy to sprout a number of different seeds to eat. They are crisp, juicy and nutty eaten raw in salads and large seeds, such as mung beans, are used in stir-fried meals. Although there are seed sprouters available, you don't actually need any special equipment. Experiment with different seeds to see which is your favourite type.

you will need

- **edible seeds** (*see* Plant List)
- **sieve** (strainer)
- **glass jars**, 1 per type of seed
- **lids**, 1 per jar

---

plant list
- ✳ Aduki beans
- ✳ Alfalfa seeds
- ✳ Mung beans
- ✳ Mustard seeds

TOP TIP

▶ You can buy small packets of seed for sprouting from garden centres. They have all the instructions for each type attached, but once you know what to do it is cheaper to buy larger amounts of seeds and beans from health food stores and supermarkets.

mustard seeds

mung beans

alfalfa seeds

aduki beans

1 Pour a small quantity of seeds or beans into a sieve and rinse them thoroughly under cold running water. This removes dust or dirt. Pick out any tiny stones that you can see with your fingers.

2 Tip or scrape out the wet seeds or beans into a clean, recycled glass jar and half-fill the container with water. Slightly warm water helps the seed to swell faster. Leave overnight or for 12 hours.

3 You'll find the seeds have grown in size due to the amount of water absorbed. Some will not grow. Pick out these hard seeds. Different seed types grow at different rates.

4 Rinse the seeds again under cold running water. Tiny alfalfa seeds are easier to tap or flick out of a small, plastic-mesh tea strainer. Rinsing stops sprouts going mouldy.

5 Drain, shaking off excess water and transfer the seeds to a clean jar. Stand out of direct sunlight but not in the dark. Cover loosely with a lid to stop the air in the jar drying out too much.

6 You'll start to see the seeds sprout, pushing out roots. Rinse, drain and return to the rinsed-out jars every 8–12 hours. It takes the sprouts around 2–4 days to grow big enough to eat.

Plants from seeds

Would you like to know what the plant that produces your favourite type of fruit looks like? It's worth trying any kind of fruit seed, not only the ones on the list below, just for the challenge of seeing if you can get them to grow.

you will need

- **fresh, ripe fruits** (see Fruit List)
- **chopping board**
- **sharp knife**
- **sieve (strainer)**
- **small plant** or **plastic pots**, such as yogurt containers
- **scissors**
- **peat-free seed** and **cutting compost (soil mix)**
- **tray** or **bowl**
- **plastic bags**
- **slender canes (stakes)**
- **elastic (rubber) bands**
- **damp sand**
- **plant labels**

fruit list
- ✳ Apple
- ✳ Avocado
- ✳ Grapefruit
- ✳ Kumquat
- ✳ Lemon
- ✳ Lime
- ✳ Orange
- ✳ Passion fruit

FACT FILE

ORANGES AND LEMONS

You can grow lots of different members of the citrus family from seed — orange, lemon, lime, grapefruit and kumquat. Most of the seedlings won't grow fruit but they make fun houseplants anyway. Crush a leaf and you'll smell the orange, lemon or whatever fruit the seed came from really strongly.

oranges and lemons

1 Cut your chosen fruits in half on a chopping board using a sharp knife. Take great care and always cut downwards on to a non-slip surface. You may need adult supervision.

2 Pick out the seeds and rinse off any juice or fruit pulp by putting the seeds in a sieve and holding them under running water. The sugars in the fruit juice can cause mould to grow.

3 Gather a few small plant pots or old food containers. Make holes in the bottom of the pots for drainage with scissors, with adult supervision. Fill with compost and firm lightly.

4 Push the lemon seeds a little way down into the compost with your finger. Cover lightly with compost, stand the pots in a bowl of tepid water for half an hour, then drain.

5 Put plastic bags over the pots with canes to hold them up and secure with an elastic band. Place on a well-lit windowsill. The plastic bag acts like a mini greenhouse. Pot on when seedlings have grown.

6 Apple seeds usually need a cold snap before they will germinate. Take the seeds out of the core, mix them with some damp sand and keep in the refrigerator for 6–8 weeks before sowing outdoors.

 ! = Watch out! Sharp or dangerous tool in use.   = Watch out! Adult help is needed.

7 To grow an avocado pear tree, extract the stone (pit) and clean it. Plant in a pot of compost so that the bottom half is buried. The base of the seed has a crease or wrinkle.

8 After watering, put the avocado somewhere warm, such as an airing cupboard or other warm area to start the germination. The seed will start to crack. Move to a warm, well-lit windowsill and eventually pot on (prick out).

TOP TIP
▶ Always remember to label pots with the name of the plant and the date you sowed the seeds, so you don't get confused.

Saucer veg

Farmers usually cut off the growing tops of root vegetables before shipping them off to the shops, so you don't normally see what the leaves look like. In this project the leaves spring back to life!

you will *need*
- **fresh-looking root vegetable selection** (*see* Vegetable List)
- **sharp knife**
- **chopping board**
- **saucers**
- **small watering can**
- **sand** (optional)

vegetable list
- ✳ **Beetroot (beet)**
- ✳ **Carrot**
- ✳ **Parsnip**
- ✳ **Radish**
- ✳ **Swede (rutabaga)**
- ✳ **Sweet potato**
- ✳ **Turnip**

FACT FILE

TAPROOTS

Although the vegetables listed vary in shape, they are all kinds of taproot, which is where the plant stores food and water.

turnips

1 Try to select very fresh-looking root vegetables, perhaps ones that still have leaves on or that have clusters of green buds at the top. Ones that you have grown in the garden would be ideal! Wash off any soil or dirt under cold running water.

2 Ask an adult to help you cut the tops off the vegetables using a sharp knife and cutting down on to a chopping board. Cut about 2.5cm/1in away from the top, so you have a chunky piece with a flat base. Trim off any leaves, but leave any buds.

3 Allow the cut surfaces of the vegetables to dry off for a day in a cool place. Next, place the vegetable tops, cut-side down, on saucers and put them close to a light window. Add a small amount of water to the saucer with a watering can.

4 Change the water every day. Rinse the saucer and vegetable tops in running water and discard any pieces that have started to rot. After a while, leaves will appear out of the tops.

5 When the vegetable tops have several leaves they can dry out more quickly, especially on sunny days, so it is important to top them up with water regularly. An alternative way to grow the tops is in saucers filled with moist sand.

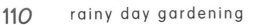 = Watch out! Sharp or dangerous tool in use.   = Watch out! Adult help is needed.

Hyacinth in a glass

Hyacinths are very pretty and smell gorgeous. Growing them in clear glass bulb vases allows you to see the roots develop and it's exciting to watch the flower-bud slowly push through.

you will need

- **bulb vases**
- **pebbles** (optional)
- **prepared hyacinth bulbs**
- **charcoal chips**

TOP TIP

▶ Like prepared hyacinths, paper white daffodils will also root in water. Fill a glass bowl with small pebbles or beads. Plant groups of 5 or 10 bulbs, pointed end up, then add water to just below the bulb base. Keep dark for 2–3 weeks.

paper white daffodils

1 Fill the bulb vases with water to a level that is just below the cup-shaped bulb holder, where the vase is narrowest. Vases come in different designs and colours. Some are larger and straight-sided, in which case use pebbles to support the bulbs above water.

2 Ordinary hyacinth bulbs won't work for early indoor display. Instead, you need to use prepared ones that have been treated with a period of cold to mimic winter, which activates them. You can buy these from a garden centre.

3 Place a bulb, pointed end upwards, in the top of each container. You may want to wear gloves – they can irritate. Make sure the bulb is not sitting in direct contact with the water or it may rot. Place in a dark, cool place, around 9°C/48°F, such as a pantry or garage.

4 Move the hyacinths from the dark place into a warm, lightly shaded spot once the shoot tip has grown to around 4–5cm/ 1½–2in. Gradually introduce more light over the next few days. Charcoal chips keep the water fresh, so there is no need to change it.

Grass head man

This character can be made at any time of year and will spring into growth in just a few days. The fun continues as the grass 'hair' grows, letting you snip a variety of styles.

you will need
- **old pair** of **tights** or **stockings**
- **scissors**
- **grass seed**
- **peat-free potting compost (soil mix)**
- **small, coloured elastic (rubber) bands**, 3
- **self-adhesive eyes**, 2
- **container**
- **saucer** or **dish**
- **small watering can**

TOP TIP
▶ To really soak the compost well, stand the figure in a container of water and wait for the compost to turn dark.

1 Cut off the foot section of an old pair of tights or stockings. You'll need a piece roughly 30cm/12in long. Hold the 'toe' open and put in about a dessert spoon of grass seed.

2 Add some potting compost to form the bulk of the head.

3 Press the compost down. Knot the top of the stocking. Trim away any excess with scissors. Adult supervision is required.

4 Form the nose by drawing out a lump of compost. Keep this in place with an elastic band. Repeat for the ears.

5 All the face needs now to bring it to life is a pair of eyes. Stick them on without being too neat. Wonky eyes add character!

6 After soaking (see Top Tip) stand on a dish on a windowsill. In a few days you will start to see the grass seed germinate.

7 Once a decent head of hair has grown, trim it with scissors to form a flat top, if you like.

8 Water the hair as needed with a small watering can. On warm sunny days, pour extra water into the saucer to act as a reservoir.

(!) = Watch out! Sharp or dangerous tool in use. (☜) = Watch out! Adult help is needed.

Potato pets

It doesn't take long to make these cute potato pets. Try using different sizes of potato to create a family. Cut the mustard or cress for salads and re-sow on a new pad.

you will need
- potato peeler
- flat-bottomed baking potato, 1–2
- thick wire
- wire cutters, secateurs or pruners
- craft foam
- double-sided adhesive tape
- coloured pompons or balls, 1–2
- self-adhesive eyes, 2–4
- kitchen paper
- small watering can
- mustard or cress seed

TOP TIP
► Keep the kitchen paper moist, adding a little splash of water every day, but don't fill the potato reservoir with water or it may start to rot.

1 Use a potato peeler to carefully carve out a shallow indent in the top of a potato. Adult supervision is required. Repeat with a second potato if you like.

2 Ask an adult to cut the wire into short lengths with wire cutters or secateurs, then bend into pin shapes.

3 Make the snout using a square of craft foam, folding it into a cone and securing with double-sided adhesive tape. Attach to the potato with wire.

4 Add a pompon nose to the end of the snout using a small piece of folded double-sided tape.

5 Attach the eyes above where the snout joins the potato. Make a pair of ears from small circles of foam with a flat base. Use wire pins to form the ear shape and attach to the potato.

6 Line the carved-out indent with a piece of folded up kitchen paper.

7 Moisten the kitchen paper with water. Mustard or cress seeds germinate quickly and only need a damp surface to start them off. Sprinkle the seeds on to the paper.

8 Stand your pets on a windowsill and watch their 'fur' grow.

Weird and wacky plants

The houseplants in this collection, including the cockscomb featured in the main picture, are some of the most bizarre, both in the way they look as well as how they live in the wild. They include meat-eating plants, plants that have no roots, plants that catch and store their own water supply in a leafy vase, and plants that can rapidly move their leaves and branches if danger threatens!

you will need
- **selection** of **plants** (see Plant List)
- **plant mister**
- **shallow pot**
- **tray**
- **gravel** or **coloured glass**, **acrylic chips** or **gravel**
- **small watering can**
- **piece** of **wire**

sensitive plant

pitcher plant

FACT FILE

AIR PLANTS
Scientists call these amazingly tough plants bromeliads, but they get their common name from the fact that many grow on tree branches (such as Spanish moss) and seem to live on nothing but humid air and rainwater. The pineapple on page 204 is a bromeliad that grows in the ground.

flowering guzmania

plant list
* **Bead plant, pin chushion**
  Nertera granadensis
* **Blushing bromeliad**
  Neoregelia carolinae 'Tricolor'
* **Common cockscomb**
  Celosia argentea var. cristata
* **Guzmania**
  Guzmania 'Yellow Marjan'
* **Pitcher plant**
  Sarracenia purpurea
* **Sensitive plant, touch-me-not**
  Mimosa pudica
* **Spanish moss**
  Tillandsia usneoides

1 Have you ever seen a plant move in front of your eyes? Gently touch the leaves of the sensitive plant and watch them fold together. A bigger nudge makes the branches droop!

2 In the wild, Spanish moss hangs from tree branches in soft grey curtains. It has no roots and lives by absorbing moisture from the air. Hang from a wire hook and spray with rainwater.

3 The cockscomb is a tender annual plant with the strangest looking folded flowers. Discover how furry the crinkled heads feel by gently stroking them with your finger.

4 Both the guzmania and neoregelia are tree-dwelling bromeliads, able to collect rainwater in their leafy vases. Keep them happy on a tray of moist gravel or glass chips.

ⓘ = Watch out! Sharp or dangerous tool in use.   ☻ = Watch out! Adult help is needed.

5 Water these plants into the base of the leaves using a narrow-spouted watering can and rainwater. Keep the gravel tray filled with water but don't let the base of the pot stand in water.

6 This pitcher plant snacks on flies caught in its leaf traps. Once inside, the fly is slowly digested! Stand on a gravel tray and keep the mossy compost moist with rainwater.

7 This bead plant from South America produces a carpet of orange bead-like fruits. Gently touch the surface to feel how hard they are. Always water from the bottom.

FACT FILE
AIR PONDS
Some tropical frogs reproduce in the mini ponds created by the vase-shaped leaves of some tree and ground-dwelling air plants.

Mini glasshouse garden

Welcome to the world of glass gardens! Even if you don't have an outside space, it is possible to create your own mini garden indoors in a glass container. Here, a special container called a terrarium is used, but you could also use a large glass jar that has a lid.

you will need
- **selection** of **houseplant tots** (*see* Plant List)
- **bucket** of **water**
- **terrarium**
- **gravel**
- **trowel**
- **houseplant compost**
- **glass decorations**, **wood** or **a shell**
- **small watering can**

FACT FILE

PERFECT PLANTS

Garden centres often have little tots or baby houseplants for sale, which are very cheap and will fit inside the miniature glasshouse. Houseplants that enjoy constant warmth and humidity and that are slow-growing and compact are ideal for terrariums and bottle gardens as they will not outgrow them too quickly. The types listed in the Plant List can all be used, so choose the ones you like best.

baby houseplants

plant list
- **Aluminium plant**
  Pilea cadierei
- **Baby rubber plant**
  Peperomia obtusifolia variegated form
- **Creeping moss**
  Selaginella martensii
- **Croton**
  Codiaeum variegatum var. *pictum* 'Gold Dust'
- **Dragon tree**
  Dracaena marginata 'Tricolor'
- **Parlour palm**
  Neanthe bella
- **Polka dot plant, freckle face**
  Hypoestes phyllostachya
- **Silver lace fern**
  Pteris ensiformis
- **Spider aralia, false aralia**
  Dizygotheca elegantissima

1 Plunge the plants in a bucket of water and wait until the bubbles stop. Put 2.5cm/1in of gravel in the bottom of the terrarium. Larger containers need more gravel.

2 Using a trowel, scoop up compost to transfer to the terrarium. You can fill to the bottom of the door and, if necessary, make the compost deeper towards the back.

3 Firm the compost slightly with your hand, then start planting the taller plants such as the dragon tree first, as this will go in towards the back or centre of the terrarium.

4 Put in the spider aralia next, followed by the polka dot plant. Try to place the plants to give them space to grow and to create as much contrast as possible in leaf shape and colour.

(!) = Watch out! Sharp or dangerous tool in use.　　(🐾) = Watch out! Adult help is needed.

5 The bright, golden leaves of this croton will add a splash of colour. When you look through the terrarium door it's like looking into a miniature forest of fantasy trees.

6 The rounded leaves of a cream variegated peperomia at the front of the terrarium contrast well with the spiky leaves of the dragon tree. Firm the plants in lightly with your fingers.

7 Make a kind of pathway through the plants, adding some extra colour with glass beads or, for a more natural look, add some aquarium driftwood or perhaps a shell.

8 Position the terrarium out of direct sunlight. Water very sparingly as it is easy to make the compost and plants too wet, which can lead to problems. Keep the door closed to make it more humid.

glass decorations

mini glasshouse garden   117

Safari garden

This indoor garden creates an exciting setting for your zoo animals. We've chosen a safari theme based around a watering hole in the African savannah, but you could just as easily create a steamy jungle with monkeys, snakes and jaguars. All the plants and the pool fit into a waterproof tray, which can be placed on a tabletop close to a window. Water very sparingly when the compost looks a little dry and mist with a sprayer.

you will need

- **houseplant compost (soil mix)**
- **waterproof container,** such as a sterilized cat litter tray
- **trowel**
- **aluminium foil**
- **houseplant tots** (see Plant List)
- **bucket** of **water**
- **shallow dish** of **water**
- **mist sprayer**
- **pebbles**
- **plastic safari animals**
- **narrow-spouted watering can**

plastic lion

TOP TIP

▶ If you don't have a waterproof container, use a black refuse (garbage) bag to line a shallow fruit box or crate. Alternatively, to ensure your garden has good drainage, find a large plastic tray to sit the box on. If you line the box with plastic, put some holes in the base.

wooden crate

plant list

✳ **Bead plant**
  Nertera granadensis
✳ **Delta maidenhair, maidenhair fern**
  Adiantum raddianum
✳ **Dragon tree, pineapple plant**
  Dracaena 'Janet Craig Compacta'
✳ **Pink quill, air plant**
  Tillandsia cyanea
✳ **Ribbon plant, lucky bamboo**
  Dracaena sanderiana

pink quill

1 Put some compost in a container using a trowel, banking it up towards the edges and making a space in the middle for the pool. Scrunch the edges of a piece of foil to make an oval shape.

2 Plunge the houseplant tots in a bucket of water and wait for the bubbles to stop. Water the bead plant by standing it in a shallow dish of water. Plant the three ribbon plants.

3 Balance the mini forest with an airy delta maidenhair fern. All indoor ferns like being misted with tepid water from a hand sprayer to keep the leaves from drying out.

4 The dramatic rosette-shaped dragon tree can go in next. Dragon trees are normally quite tall but this will stay neat and compact. With its dark glossy leaves feels totally tropical!

⚠ = Watch out! Sharp or dangerous tool in use.   🦁 = Watch out! Adult help is needed.

5 Bead plants are low carpeting species producing bright orange fruits. Dig out a hole for the roots with your hand and plant so that it can grow over the edge.

6 To make it feel even more like the lush vegetation surrounding a watering hole, plant a pink quill plant. Add pebbles around the pool to look like boulders.

7 Start to add your animals – whatever African savannah creatures you may have. We've put a big elephant at the front but the zebra is hiding in the trees at the back!

8 Carefully fill the pool with water from a beaker. You shouldn't need to water the plants at this stage, but you will need to in future, using a narrow-spouted watering can.

Fantasy garden

Cacti and succulents are amazing desert plants that come in all kinds of weird shapes and sizes. There are so many to choose from that it can be hard to pick out just a few plants for a collection. The ones chosen for this little fantasy garden are all easy for beginners to grow. All they need is a well-lit windowsill and only a little water. Carefully feel down with your finger into the compost and only water if it is dry.

you will need
- **crock (clay piece)** or **broken tile**
- **terracotta bulb bowl**
- **soil-based potting compost (soil mix)**
- **horticultural grit**
- **plastic mixing bowl**
- **trowel**
- **range of cacti** and **succulents**
  (see Plant List)
- **kitchen paper**
- **spoon**
- **blue acrylic mulch**
- **plastic dinosaur** or **monster**

plastic dinosaur

FACT FILE
CLEVER CACTI
Members of the cactus family naturally live in desert areas where there is very little water, high daytime temperatures and strong sunlight. To survive, they have a thick waterproof coat, spines to stop them being eaten and sometimes light-reflecting hairs, as well as swollen stems capable of storing water.

cactus

plant list
* **Echeveria species** (in flower)
* **Fishhook cactus, devil's tongue barrel**
  Ferocactus latispinus
* **Good luck plant, mother of thousands**
  Bryophyllum daigremontianum
* **Peanut cactus**
  Chamaecereus sylvestri
* **Pincushion cactus**
  Mammillaria species

WARNING – The spines of cacti can be sharp. Take great care if handling them. The *Opuntia* cactus has irritating hairs.

1 Put a piece of crock or broken tile over the drainage hole in a terracotta bulb bowl to help stop it becoming blocked with compost. Good drainage is vital for cacti and succulents.

2 Mix together potting compost and horticultural grit in a bowl, stirring the two together with a trowel. This gritty mixture will give the plant roots plenty of drainage.

3 Add some of the mixture to the bulb bowl. Carefully take the first plant out of its pot – the leaves of some succulents can be quite brittle. Sit the two echeverias side by side.

4 Work compost around the root-balls, then add the good luck plant. This easy houseplant develops tiny plantlets complete with roots along the edges of its leaves.

5 Though the peanut cactus may look prickly, it is quite soft. Plant it at the edge of the bowl and next to it add the pincushion cactus, scooping compost back around the roots.

6 To take the fishhook cactus with its fierce spines out of its pot, hold the 'head' with a piece of folded kitchen paper. Continue to hold the cactus like this during planting.

7 After filling in all the gaps round the root-balls and firming with your fingers, use a spoon to spread fine blue acrylic mulch (or any other coloured mulch) around the plants.

8 For the finishing touch, place a dinosaur or monster figure in among the plants. The bizarre cacti and funky blue glass make the perfect fantasy landscape for a dino!

fantasy garden   121

Mini farmyard

It's fun to create miniature worlds and to be able to imagine yourself walking around in them. You can put a pig in an enclosure that looks most like a muddy pigsty and settle cows, a sheep and carthorse in a mossy field. You can swap features around really easily, move and rebuild fences and pathways, create new fields, and make a twig and bark stable, perhaps, and even a corral for exercising horses. So get collecting and let your imagination run wild!

you will need
- **waterproof container**, such as a sterilized cat litter tray
- **potting compost (soil mix)**
- **trowel**
- **twigs**
- **aluminium foil**
- **grit** and **sand**
- **moss**
- **farmyard animals**
- **clippings** from **evergreens**
- **herb cuttings** and **seed-heads**

FACT FILE
BUILD A WALL
We've used horticultural grit to make our cobbled path but if you collect some larger stones, shingle pieces or small slate chippings, you could build a traditional-looking stone wall, if you prefer. You might need to glue the pieces with PVA (white) glue to make the wall a more solid.

assorted stones

TOP TIP
► If you can't find any flat moss pieces to make the field, pull some grass and shred that into small pieces to cover the compost. Alternatively, pull small leaves off green coloured shrubs or herbs and overlap them to form a carpet.

1 Half-fill a waterproof tray with some dry potting compost. This will act as a base to support some of the fences and trees later on. You can also mound it up to form hummocks.

2 Build a small square enclosure for one of your farmyard animals by putting in a line of broken-up twigs. The twigs, standing in for logs, need to be about the same length.

3 Break up some larger forked twigs so that they are the same size. Plant them, evenly spaced, in a row, then rest a long thin twig across the forks to make a fence.

4 Take a piece of foil and mould it into a shallow dish shape. Scrunch up the edges to make it more robust. Position the duck pond in one corner of the tray and fill with water.

(!) = Watch out! Sharp or dangerous tool in use.   (✂) = Watch out! Adult help is needed.

5 Carefully trickle some grit around the pigsty or pen to make a cobbled pathway. You can firm it lightly with your fingers to make it lie flatter. Use sand to make a dirt track, if you like.

6 Collect a few pieces of thin carpeting moss from wood or stone in shady parts of the garden. Create the effect of a grassy meadow by patching the pieces together.

7 Add some more animals to the pasture – a cow or two, maybe some horses and foals or make it a field of grazing sheep watched over by a sheep dog. The choice is yours!

8 Use clippings from evergreen shrubs, herb sprigs and seed-heads to create hedges and trees. Because of the scale, even a small clipping looks like a big tree!

mini farmyard   123

Ivy animals

You can buy wire topiary frames in many different designs and a small animal figure, such as this squirrel, can be made in just a couple of hours. This craft is part of a very old tradition of clipping and training plants into fun shapes called topiary. Ivy animals can be temporarily dressed up for special occasions and make great presents. Ivy is easy to grow and can take quite a lot of shade. Put on a cool windowsill out of direct sun.

you will need
- **bulb bowl** or **shallow planter**
- **crock** (clay piece)
- **peat-free potting compost** (soil mix)
- **trowel**
- **pots** of **rooted ivy** (*Hedera helix*) **cuttings**, 3
- **bucket** of **water**
- **wire mesh topiary frame**
- **pencil**
- **moist sphagnum moss**
- **pieces** of **green plastic coated wire**, 12cm/5in lengths
- **small scissors**
- **small watering can**
- **ribbon**
- **self-adhesive eyes**
- **felt nose** (optional)
- **mist sprayer**

WARNING – There is a very small chance of fungal infection from sphagnum moss. It is a good idea to wear thin latex gloves when handling moss.

TOP TIP
▶ You'll probably find many forms of English ivy (*Hedera helix*) at the garden centre or nursery, but the best for small topiary figures are ones with small, plain green leaves and only very short gaps between the leaves along the stems. These ivies stay nice and compact, are easy to train and won't overwhelm the frame.

English ivy

project equipment

1 Cover the drainage hole in the shallow bowl or pot with a piece of crock. Half-fill with compost using a trowel. Plunge the plants in a bucket of water and wait for the bubbles to stop.

2 Dig your thumbs into the centre of the ivy root-ball and open it out into a strip of cuttings. Place the strip around the edge of the prepared bulb bowl or planter.

3 Ensure you have ivies all round the edge, then add more compost to cover the roots and firm lightly with your hands. Next take the moss and start filling the wire mesh topiary frame.

4 Use a pencil to work the moss into all the hard-to-reach spaces in the frame, such as the tail. Really pack the moss in tightly as it will shrink slightly when dry and can leave gaps.

! = Watch out! Sharp or dangerous tool in use. = Watch out! Adult help is needed.

7 Trim off any leaves that stick out too far using scissors, along with any over-long shoots. Adult supervision is required. Water to moisten the compost. Tie a ribbon bow round the neck of the animal.

5 Put the frame into the centre of the pot. Start to train each long strand of ivy on to the frame using pieces of wire bent in half to make pins. Angle these in downwards when positioning.

6 Take the ivy stems around the main parts of the body, avoiding the head, and also secure them up and over the tail. Put extra pins in to keep the stems tight against the moss.

8 Pin on eyes and a felt nose, if you like. Mist the topiary figure regularly to keep the moss moist. Continue to pin new ivy growth on to the moss and trim back wayward shoots.

VARIATION
• Creeping fig (*Ficus pumila*) grows in a similar way to ivy, rooting into the moss where the shoots touch. It is not hardy and likes being misted.

Index

Acknowledgements

Author's acknowledgements
I'd like to thank all the children who took part in the photography as well as the parents, who were most helpful and patient. Special mention goes to Leslie Ingram and Viv Palmer for finding so many willing models and for allowing us to take over their homes and gardens. I'm also grateful to the other garden owners for generously providing access. So much of the success of the book is down to Howard Rice's marvellous photographs and Viv Palmer's artistic flair.

Picture credits
All pictures © Anness Publishing Ltd, apart from the following:
t = top; b = bottom; r = right;
l = left; c = centre; m = main.

Gap Photos 111m.
iStockphoto 8tr, 9tr, 10tr, 12tr, 14tr, 19tr, 20tr, 23tr, 55bl, 30cl, 32cl, 29cl, 26br, 78m, 82cl, 88cl, 88cr, 90cr, 92cl, 96cl, 98bl, 58cl, 58cr, 60cr, 64bl, 65bl, 66tr, 66cl, 66cr, 67cl, 68tr, 68cr, 70tr, 70cr, 109cl, 110cr, 111cl, 114c, 118tr, 118cl, 120cl, 122cl, 124cl,